OTTO JESPERSEN: FACETS OF HIS LIFE AND WORK

AMSTERDAM STUDIES IN THE THEORY AND

HISTORY OF LINGUISTIC SCIENCE

General Editor
E. F. KONRAD KOERNER
(University of Ottawa)

Series III - STUDIES IN THE HISTORY OF THE LANGUAGE SCIENCES

Advisory Editorial Board

Ranko Bugarski (Belgrade); Jean-Claude Chevalier (Paris)
H.H. Christmann (Tübingen); Boyd H. Davis (Charlotte, N.C.)
Rudolf Engler (Bern); Hans-Josef Niederehe (Trier)
R.H. Robins (London); Rosane Rocher (Philadelphia)
Vivian Salmon (Oxford); Aldo Scaglione (New York)

Volume 52

Arne Juul and Hans F. Nielsen (eds)

Otto Jespersen:
Facets of his Life and Work

OTTO JESPERSEN
FACETS OF HIS LIFE AND WORK

Edited by

ARNE JUUL and HANS F. NIELSEN
Royal Danish School   *Odense University*
of Educational Studies

JOHN BENJAMINS PUBLISHING COMPANY
AMSTERDAM/PHILADELPHIA

1989

ROBERT MANNING
STROZIER LIBRARY

FEB 13 1990

Tallahassee, Florida

P
85
J4
088
1989

Library of Congress Cataloging in Publication Data

Otto Jespersen: facets of his life and work / edited by Arne Juul and Hans F. Nielsen.
    p.   cm. -- (Amsterdam studies in the theory and history of linguistic science. Series III, Studies in the history of the language sciences, ISSN 0304-0720; v. 52)
Includes bibliographical references.
1. Jespersen, Otto, 1860-1943. 2. Linguists -- Denmark -- Biography. I. Juul, Arne. II. Nielsen, Hans Frede, 1943-   . III. Series.
P85.J4088   1989
410'.92 -- dc20
[B]   89-17797
ISBN 90 272 4537 1 (alk. paper)   CIP

© Copyright 1989 - John Benjamins B.V.
No part of this book may be reproduced in any form, by print, photoprint, microfilm, or any other means, without written permission from the publisher.

CONTENTS

Facets of Otto Jespersen (c. 1915). Multiple image by mirror, Copenhagen. By courtesy of the Royal Library, Copenhagen.

Randolph Quirk

PREFACE

Tennyson's *In Memoriam*, whose very title it is fitting to recall on this occasion, contains the stanza

> I care not in these fading days
> > To raise a cry that lasts not long,
> > And round thee with the breeze of song
> To stir a little dust of praise.

'I care not', because one of the remarkable facts about Jespersen is that the value of his writings has never shown signs of fading, and his insights continue to stir more than 'a little dust of praise' among students of many languages and of many different theoretical persuasions around the world.

But *In Memoriam* serves as a good starting point for another reason. It is a poem from which Jespersen himself quoted in one of his best known and best loved books, *Growth and Structure*, to make the claim that

> words, like Nature, half reveal
> And half conceal the Soul within.

Of the contributors to the present volume, I think only Paul Christophersen had the privileged degree of face-to-face acquaintance that could reveal Jespersen's personality and something of the 'Soul within'. But all the other writers here assembled, along with the countless thousands who continue to draw inspiration from his work, feel as they read him that they are in touch with a warm and lively man, as full of concern for humanity itself as for what he saw as the key to humanity, the faculty of language.

The two of course go together and he would not perhaps himself have recognised the distinction. Nonetheless it was the humane concern rather than the scientific that led him to devote so much of his enthusiastic energy to reform in the teaching of modern languages: with enormously influential results, as Knud Sørensen shows below – and not by any means only in Denmark. So too it was his idealism that drove him to make major explorations in devising means to facilitate international communication, even though 'towards the end of his life' he 'expressed some qualms about the time and energy he had invested in these projects'.

But even in areas such as these where the battle has either been won (as in teaching languages with emphasis on practical speech) or largely abandoned (as in this particular mode of artificial language), his work will go on repaying further study. The same can be said – even more emphatically – about his work on linguistic theory, such as his excellent 1917 study of negation and especially perhaps the reflective and challenging *Philosophy of Grammar* (1924), with his views put in a still broader context the following year in *Mankind, Nation and Individual*. Nor should we forget the more cryptic book a dozen years later, the *Analytic Syntax*, which he seems to have regarded as his last word on the distinctive aspects of his linguistic theory.

But for the majority of us, the work to which we have most frequent recourse, the work that stands out as being most irreplaceable, is the monumental seven volumes of *A Modern English Grammar*. With its wide range of data from literature of all periods and the illuminating explanatory comment, simultaneously along diachronic and synchronic dimensions, this book is a continual source of inspiration and value. It more than 'half reveals' what is specific to Jespersen – his Anglophil romanticism and belief in linguistic progress discussed below by Hans Frede Nielsen, for example – without our needing to fear that his scholarly judgment is ever relaxed, still less distorted. Whatever our occasional exasperation as we try to find our way through a work that was many decades in the making, the search is always rewarding. Nelson Francis tells us that he has 'frequently had the experience of hitting upon what I thought was an original idea, only to find on checking that Jespersen had been there before me'. It is not just *MEG* that produces, and will go on producing, this effect on generations of students.

ACKNOWLEDGEMENTS

The editors wish to express their gratitude to friends, colleagues and institutions for their kindness and their help. In particular:

British Library
Danmarks Radio
The Library of the Royal Danish School of Educational Studies
The National Library of Education, Copenhagen
The National Sound Archive, Copenhagen
Odense University Library
The Royal Library, Copenhagen,
The Royal Library, Stockholm

for their goodwill and their unfailing patience. We are also most grateful to:

The British Council
The Carlsberg Foundation
Copenhagen University
The Danish Research Council for the Humanities
The Ministry of Education, International Relations Division
The National Institute for Educational Media, Copenhagen
Odense University
The Royal Danish School of Educational Studies

for their generous support in countless ways.

We would like to thank the following: Paul Christophersen, Cambridge; Arne S. Arnesen, Hans Berggreen and Ruth Bentzen of the Royal Library, Copenhagen, for never having failed to respond constructively whenever we needed expert help; Leif Grane and Anne Vibeke Vad of

Acknowledgements

Regensen, Copenhagen, for their kind assistance while we were hunting for photographs of Jespersen from his time at Regensen; D. Yde-Andersen and Ebba Dahlstrøm of the National Sound Archive and Poul v. Linstow of Danmarks Radio for their indefatigable efforts to help us in our attemps to find early recordings of Jespersen; and especially E. F. K. Koerner of the University of Ottawa and John Benjamins Publishers for kindly accepting this book for publication in the SiHOLS series.

A final word of thanks to Peter Collier, Pangbourne, to Povl Skårup and Knud Sørensen, Aarhus University, to David Stoner, Bromley, and to Bent Sunesen, Charlottenlund, for their editorial comments and to Henny Eriksen and Birthe Færing, Odense University, for their outstanding secretarial help.

EDITORS' INTRODUCTION

One day in the spring of 1985, while working on *Our Changing Speech. Two BBC Talks by Daniel Jones*, which was published later that year,[1] we began to wonder why recordings of Otto Jespersen's voice appear to be so rare today. Whereas Jones's voice has been left for posterity in a variety of recordings,[2] we seem to have only three recordings of Jespersen (1903, 1913 and 1941).

This regrettable fact reminds us of what David Lance said a few years ago in a publication on sound archives:

> Until quite recently, ... the relationship between sound recording and historical documentation was haphazard. Most collected material had been recorded – often by broadcasting organisations – for immediate practical ends. Any subsequent preservation by archivists aware of its permanent historical value was generally incidental to the reasons for which the recordings were originally made. In the field of historical sound documentation – as with many other classes of records – archival collections, therefore, traditionally consisted of recordings that were created without objective regard to historical considerations and which survived, very often, only by accident and good fortune.[3]

Jespersen was 65 years old when broadcasting on a regular basis began in Denmark in 1925. It has proved impossible to ascertain the extent to which his voice was recorded by Danmarks Radio over the following eighteen years. What we do know is that, strange as it may seem, only one interview exists in Danmarks Radio's Sound Archives. By the irony of fate, the voice of the Danish phonetician *par excellence* only just survives.

In 1938, five years before his death, the 78-year-old Jespersen looked back. It is true that nowhere in his autobiography, *En sprogmands levned*, does Jespersen mention recordings of his own voice and on the whole he says very little about sound recording. But he was certainly an ardent advocate of the then embryonic *talemuseer* ('speech museums'), as he called them: in the recording from 1913, as we pointed out in 1985, Jespersen recommended that sound archives should be established in which linguists and others would be able to study voices of the past.[4]

We consequently decided to see to it that at least two of the recordings (1913 and 1941) would be made available to the general public in Denmark and abroad. The recordings will be published separately by the National Institute for Educational Media together with an introduction by one of the contributors to the present volume, Paul Christophersen.[5]

A further outcome of our considerations was the idea of publishing a book on Jespersen which would enable students and scholars to receive a detailed impression of some important facets of the Dane who is still a household name in the world of linguistics. And it seemed natural to let the book begin with the general introduction by Paul Christophersen, who knew Jespersen well.

Jespersen was enormously productive. A complete bibliography exists in two parts: the first covering the period from 1883 to 1930;[6] the second the period from 1930 to 1943.[7] The total number of publications listed here is 487.

How did he manage to do all this while at the same time – as once observed by Christophersen – he 'never seemed in a hurry and always had time for visitors'?[8]

Jespersen himself would no doubt have answered that he was simply unable to bridle his passion for intellectual activity. In 1938, several years after he had retired from Copenhagen University, he remarked that had he not written a single word after 1925, nobody would have blamed him, and he asked himself why he had kept on working. Perhaps, he said, because working had become an inveterate habit, as indispensable as the hypodermic needle to the morphine addict. He continued:

> With me, thinking may have become a chronic disease. There is some truth in what Oscar Wilde says, 'Thinking is the most unhealthy thing in the world' (Intentions 4), and in Bertrand Russell's words: 'Thinking is not one of the natural activities of man; it is the product of disease, like a high temperature in illness' (Freedom and Org. 93).[9]

Christophersen has drawn attention to other important factors behind Jespersen's impressive list of publications, such as his working method (cf. Jespersen's 'little slips of paper' described below, p. 8) and his working conditions, in particular the financial support from the Carlsberg Foundation at the end of his career, enabling him to concentrate his efforts on *A Modern English Grammar* and other major projects.[10]

Finally, a few words about the illustrations:

It is only natural that a book on Jespersen should contain photographs, and we originally intended to present a substantial number of pictures collected from a variety of sources. Since we are, however, currently preparing an English translation of Jespersen's autobiography, we have deemed it more appropriate to reserve the majority of illustrations for that purpose.

Like the articles, the photographs in the present volume speak for themselves. But perhaps one of them deserves special mention.

It has been said of Julia Margaret Cameron, one of the pioneers in nineteenth-century British photography, that she 'had the real artist's gift of piercing through the outward appearance to the soul of the individual ...' although the impressiveness of her portraits 'in some cases undoubtedly owes much to the strong personality of her sitter'.[11] It seems to us that this statement could also be said to apply to Heinrich (Henry) Carl Hugo Buergel Goodwin (1878-1931), the artist behind the intense portrait of the vigilant 47-year-old Jespersen.[12] Goodwin, who began his career as a philologist and ended up an exceptional photographer, had been fascinated by photography in his youth and apparently met Jespersen at Ermelundsly[13] in 1907. This was at a time when Goodwin was working on phonetics and the psychology of language and only a few years before he published two articles on the idea of an international language. Whatever may have been the occasion of this meeting between two extraordinary personalities having interests in common, an outstanding result lives on in the world of art.

Frederiksberg and Sorø
January 1989

Notes

1. Juul & Nielsen (eds.) 1985.
2. See the discography in Abercrombie *et al.* 1964:xviii-xix.
3. Lance 1983:177.
4. See Juul & Nielsen (eds.) 1985:ix.
5. Further information is available from the National Institute for Educational Media (Landscentralen for Undervisningsmidler), Ørnevej 30, DK-2400 Copenhagen NV. Tel. (+45) 31 10 77 33.
6. Bodelsen 1930.
7. Haislund 1944.
8. Christophersen 1972:18.
9. Jespersen 1938:224 (our translation).
10. Christophersen 1972:18.
11. Gernsheim 1965:124.
12. For further information on Goodwin, see *Svenskt biografiskt lexikon* (1918-), Wigh 1984 and Auer 1985.
13. For Ermelundsly, see below, p. 20.

Bibliography

Abercrombie, D., D. B. Fry, P. A. D. MacCarthy, N. C. Scott and J. L. M. Trim (eds.). 1964. *In Honour of Daniel Jones*. London: Longmans.

Auer, M. & M. 1985. *Encyclopédie internationale des photographes de 1839 à nos jours / Photographers encyclopedia international 1839 to the present*. Hermance, Geneva: Editions Camera Obscura.

Bodelsen, C. A. 1930. 'Bibliography'. In: Bøgholm *et al.* (eds.) 1930, pp. 433-57.

Bøgholm, N., Aa. Brusendorff and C. A. Bodelsen (eds.). 1930. *A Grammatical Miscellany Offered to Otto Jespersen on His Seventieth Birthday*. Copenhagen: Levin & Munksgaard.

Christophersen, P. 1972. 'Otto Jespersen: A Retrospect'. *Transactions of the Philological Society*.

Frozen Image, The. Scandinavian Photography. 1984. New York: Abbeville Press.

Gernsheim, H. & A. 1965. *A concise history of photography*. London: Thames and Hudson.

Haislund, N. 1944. 'Bibliografi over Arbejder af Otto Jespersen 1930-43'. In: *Kgl. Danske Videnskabernes Selskab, Det. Oversigt over Selskabets Virksomhed Juni 1943 – Maj 1944*, pp. 57-63.

Jespersen, O. 1903. Recording. (Private collection.)

Jespersen, O. 1913. Recording ('Talt i Grammofon den 18de September 1913 af Professor Otto Jespersen'). Archive recording No. 647. The National Sound Archive (Nationalmuseets Audiovisuelle Samlinger), Copenhagen.

Jespersen, O. 1938. *En sprogmands levned*. Copenhagen: Gyldendal.

Jespersen, O. 1941. Recording of interview: 'Professor dr. phil. Otto Jespersen: Børnenes sprogtilegnelse'. Archive recording No. 0000 414. Danmarks Radio.

Juul, A. and H. F. Nielsen (eds.). 1985. *Our Changing Speech. Two BBC Talks by Daniel Jones.* (With accompanying tapes.) Copenhagen: The National Institute for Educational Media (Landscentralen for Undervisningsmidler).

Kgl. Danske Videnskabernes Selskab, Det. Oversigt over Selskabets Virksomhed Juni 1943 – Maj 1944. Copenhagen.

Lance, D. (ed.). 1983. *Sound Archives. A Guide to their Establishment and Development.* International Association of Sound Archives. Special Publication No. 4.

Svenskt biografiskt lexikon (1918-). Stockholm: Bonnier.

Wigh, L. 1984. 'Henry B. Goodwin's Women'. In: *The Frozen Image. Scandinavian Photography*, pp. 98-100.

Paul Christophersen

OTTO JESPERSEN

The first time that Otto Jespersen may be said to have come into my life was in 1922. In that year I started learning English in school, and naturally we used Jespersen and Sarauw's English primer. This book, published in 1895, continued in general use in Denmark for many years, and several generations of Danes owe their introduction to English to Jespersen's book and to the rhyme with which it began:

> I can hop, I can run.
> See me hop, see me run.
> It is fun, fun, fun.

Originally this book represented something entirely new in language teaching. When one looks at it now – and I still possess a copy – the illustrations understandably strike one as very old-fashioned, but in other respects the book is still surprisingly modern in its approach and possibly better than some of the things that have since appeared on the market.

The most revolutionary feature of the book is its use of phonetic transcription. The texts are given throughout in both ordinary orthography and phonetic script, facing each other on alternate pages, and for the first few weeks, I remember, we were only allowed to look at the phonetic script while we practised the various new sounds, a *w* and a tongue-tip *r* and a dark *l*, and generally accustomed ourselves to the sound of English. Nowadays, with radio and TV and films and cassette recordings, there is infinitely more opportunity for foreign learners to hear normal English speech than there was in those days. Even so, I think, phonetic transcription has by no means outlived its importance.

1

Phonetics engaged Jespersen's attention a great deal as a young man. Later he switched to other areas of linguistic study, and it is amazing how many different areas he managed to cover and to write about in the course of his long life. To the end, however, he was interested in speech sounds. I spent the Christmas of 1939 in London, where I met a number of students from different countries; when I told Jespersen about this in a letter, he wrote back and said, 'How I would have enjoyed this in my youth ... I would have revelled in the possibility of hearing the sounds of all those languages. But that sort of thing, I imagine, doesn't interest you so much'. I think Jespersen did me an injustice there, although my interest in phonetics may not range so widely as his.

It is not always realized that in his youth Jespersen was regarded primarily as a phonetician, and his contribution to the study of general phonetics is in fact considerable. His great textbook on the subject appeared in a Danish edition in the 1890s and in German in 1904. Jespersen has also written about the phonetics of Danish, for the study of which he prepared a special system of notation, and Danish phonetic terminology is largely his invention. Nevertheless, interest in the practical application of phonetics to the teaching of foreign languages was not peculiar to Jespersen. He shared it with various contemporaries, members of the European movement for a reform of language teaching in the 1880s and 1890s. The pioneer in this field was the Englishman Henry Sweet, to whom Jespersen looked as a shining example. Jespersen's participation in this work was an example of how his mind was open to new ideas. By temperament he was a reformer.

Let me return for a moment to Jespersen's English primer. The way grammar is smuggled in gradually is an example of the new approach to language learning that was being advocated at the time, the so-called Direct Method. In one respect, though, I think Jespersen introduced something essentially new. He uses a number of English nursery rhymes in his book: 'Doctor Foster went to Gloucester' and 'Ding, dong, bell, Puss is in the well' and 'Little Jack Horner sat in a corner', and so on. A basic idea in the Direct Method is the close link between a language and the thoughts and emotions and general culture of its speakers. This is where nursery rhymes come in; they are part of the common heritage of the nation and are often echoed or reflected in its literature. Early exposure to them is important.

Children seldom notice the names of the authors of their schoolbooks but on a certain occasion somebody in our class asked the teacher, 'Why do we keep getting stories about Robin Redbreast? Why don't we hear something about other birds?' and I suggested, 'Perhaps the author doesn't know any other English bird names'. The teacher laughed and said, 'You mustn't say that. Otto Jespersen is our great expert on the English language'. That was the first time I heard his name mentioned and had my attention drawn to him.

The next time I came across Jespersen's name was a few years later, in the third or fourth form of the Middle School. I had become interested in artificial languages, especially Ido, which in those days appeared to be the latest product of that kind, a sort of reformed Esperanto. Jespersen had taken an active part in the launching of this language; he was on an international committee which approved it in 1907, and he had written a good deal about it. I got together all the literature about Ido that I could lay hands on, in Danish and other languages, and again and again I came upon Jespersen's name. From then on I learnt to see him in his proper light, as the internationally known personality and authority that he was.

A couple of years later, in 1928, while I was at the Gymnasium stage in school, Jespersen put forward his own version of an artificial language, Novial, and I at once bought all the literature on the subject that I could get hold of and swallowed it avidly. I doubt if Novial ever gained more than a few hundred adherents, although for some years in the 1930s there was a journal, *Novialiste*, published in Sweden; the war, I think, put an end to it. Towards the end of his life Jespersen himself, I think, came to regret all the time that he had devoted to the movement for an artificial international language; it was as if he had ceased to believe in the idea. But the fact that it engaged him so strongly over such a long period of time is significant for an understanding of his character and temperament.

Jespersen was an idealist and a pacifist. In January 1940, when I was in England, I had a letter from him expressing 'deep despair over the political situation in the world'. And his last words in that letter, the last that I ever received from him, was, 'Why cannot people live in peace together!'. By temperament he was a rationalist and considered that international problems could and should be solved by an appeal to reason. Such a mode of thought and expression seems no longer to belong to our age, and spiritually Jespersen would probably have been more at home in the Age of Enlightenment. It is typical of his approach that in order to decide among the various proposed artificial languages, and to select the most suitable vocabulary for such a language, Jespersen put forward a formula based on Jeremy Bentham's utilitarian principle of morality: 'that international language is the best which on every point offers the greatest facility to the greatest number'. He advocated this principle on several occasions, and in creating his own Novial he attempted to carry it through with consistency.

Linked with Jespersen's rationalism there was his belief in progress. He owed a great debt to nineteenth-century ideas on evolution and especially to Darwin's theory of 'the survival of the fittest'. Linguistic science in the first half of the nineteenth century was characterized by the discovery of hereditary kinship among languages and of their historical development. English can be traced back to Old English, which is a branch of West Germanic, which in its turn goes back to Common Germanic, and so on and so forth, and the further back we go, the fuller is the inflexional system that we find. Old English had four or five cases, modern English has in general only two. To a romantic view of language this appeared to indicate deterioration and degeneration. We are reminded of this way of looking at the facts by the terms which the German scholar Jakob Grimm chose for the two sets of verbs in Germanic, the 'strong' and the 'weak'. The weak conjugation is a late development, which has now become the normal and regular type; but the other verbs, the old type, had far more forms, and so to Grimm they seemed to be stronger. As I said, to people of a romantic turn of mind it looked as if languages were becoming increasingly weak and impoverished. This conception was strongly contested by Jespersen: the erosion and reduction that we seem to observe may be interpreted as improvement; language is becoming simpler and easier and more flexible all the time. Jespersen put forward this view in his doctoral dissertation in 1891 and again a few years later in his book *Progress in Language*. It was also the central idea in his last book, *Efficiency in Linguistic Change* (1941). Altogether, in opposition to the romantic-historical school of linguists, Jespersen held that the modern language is an entirely worthy object of scientific study. He was one of the first to assert such a view.

Jespersen's anti-romantic personality is interestingly reflected in his prose style. As a young man he once said, 'I prefer a dry style, where the thoughts stand out sharp and clear and where emotion is allowed to shed no tears'. He was opposed to all rhetorical embellishment, probably because with his innermost being he disliked anything that savoured of posturing or standing on one's dignity. His ideal was a literary style that reflected everyday speech as closely as possible. When his wife died in 1937 and he wanted to insert an announcement in the Copenhagen dailies, he had some difficulty in persuading the conservative paper *Berlingske Tidende* to allow him to use the everyday word *kone* 'wife' rather than the more dignified term *hustru*, which is customary in that kind of context. I am not even sure that he succeeded; he told me afterwards about his difficulty, rather indignantly, and said that the radical paper, *Politiken*, had raised no objection. Besides anti-romanticism there may have been a touch of something else in Jespersen's mind over this matter. Politically his leaning was to the left in the old-fashioned sense of that word. By temperament he belonged to no party for he could never endorse any party-political platform to the full, but he was closest to the Social Democrats in their ideas about social justice, equal opportunity and the like – but not political economy, which was something that he did not concern himself with.

To return to my schooldays: the next book by Jespersen that I read at the Gymnasium stage was *Sprogets Udvikling og Opståen* ('The Evolution and Origin of Language'). Like everything else that Jespersen wrote this book fascinated me, not least by its clear exposition. Here we have another characteristic of Jespersen's literary form which deserves to be pointed out. His style was simple, but not just by the choice of words; Jespersen had a remarkable facility, a genius one might say, for presenting even the most complicated problems so that the ordinary intelligent reader could understand them. Again, I think, this is linked with Jespersen's dislike of anything that is stilted and pretentious and aimed at making the writer appear more important than he is. As Professor Bodelsen has put it: despite his apparent lack of an eye for artistic merit, by his very form of presentation Jespersen was himself an artist.

In 1930 I registered as a student of English at Copenhagen University. Jespersen was no longer there; he had retired in 1925, at the age of 65, but his influence was still felt. Both Professor Brusendorff and the latter's successor, Bodelsen, were pupils of Jespersen, and this was noticeable in various ways. We still used Jespersen's textbooks, and we were constantly reminded of his existence by the stream of new books that he poured forth. In 1931 came volume IV of his big grammar, a little too advanced for someone like myself who had only just begun his university course; but in 1933 Jespersen published *Essentials of English Grammar* and *The System of Grammar*, and they interested me greatly, so greatly that I wrote to Jespersen about a couple of points that I disagreed with. The result was an invitation to visit him at his home in Elsinore to discuss the matter, and thus began a collaboration which lasted until I went to England in 1939 to continue my studies at Cambridge. First we worked on his *Analytic Syntax* and later on volume VI of his big grammar. During those years I came to know Jespersen closely through a constant exchange of letters and numerous visits to his home, sometimes to attend lunch or dinner parties. I also received help from him of a material kind; for instance, when I got my first degree from Copenhagen he presented me with a typewriter.

I have already tried to characterize Jespersen as a person and a scholar. I should now like to summarize my remarks and add a few more. Jespersen was a reformer – not only of language teaching in the schools, but of the scholarly study of languages at the university level. A modern language, he maintained, is a fully worthy object of study, but in one's grammatical analysis one must rid oneself of the straitjacket of Latin. One must recognize that modern languages go their independent ways and follow rules of their own, often different from those of Latin and Greek. One man with whom Jespersen crossed swords on this point was the professor of classical languages at Birmingham University. He was of Austrian descent but born and educated in England, and I suppose we must anglicize the pronunciation of his name and call him Sonnen-schein [sɔnənʃaɪn] with a voiceless *s*. Now he also concerned himself with English and wrote a grammar of English in which he operated with five cases: nom. *rat*, voc. *O rat*, acc. *rat*, gen. *rat's*, dat. *rat*; and in the plural: *rats*, *O rats*, *rats*, *rats'*, and *rats*. Jespersen was fond of ridiculing absurdities like these, and all modern linguists have adopted his point of view.

When Jespersen was an undergraduate at Copenhagen, Latin was a compulsory subsidiary subject for all students of modern languages. Two subsidiary subjects were required, and Jespersen, who was taking French as his main subject, chose English as the other subsidiary. But the rule irked him considerably; all his life he was more interested in what was obviously practical and realistic, and Latin seemed to him an unnecessary treadmill; he failed to see why everybody had to be encumbered with it. It needs to be remembered, though, that the students in those days had all done Latin as a subject in school. As an undergraduate Jespersen agitated unsuccessfully for a change of the regulations; later, as a professor, he was among those responsible for abolishing compulsory Latin. I remember an occasion when Jespersen and I were talking about the waning knowledge of Latin nowadays – and let me point out that this was in the thirties, half a century after Jespersen's campaign – and I said, 'Surely it's important for a linguist to know some Latin'. Jespersen said with a smile, quoting Holberg's *Erasmus Montanus*, 'Yes, I wouldn't sell my Latin for a hundred Rigsdaler'. Whether this meant that he had changed his mind I don't know.

As part of his striving for a simple style Jespersen advocated an improved Danish orthography. Here, once again, we meet Jespersen the reformer. To use a person's ability to distinguish between *baller* and *balder* and *skylle* and *skylde* as a criterion for classifying him as educated or uneducated seemed to Jespersen to be pedantry, and Jespersen hated pedantry. He himself used a somewhat simplified Danish spelling, which on many points agrees with the currently authorized orthography.

Lack of respect for authority and tradition was an important part of Jespersen's personality. He was an iconoclast. It started, I think, as a rebellion against an ultra-conservative family tradition. For generations his ancestors had been lawyers, and he was expected to follow in their footsteps. After reading law for four years – barren years in his view – and still some distance from his finals, he suddenly changed course, sold all his law books and took up the one study that really interested him, language. In his autobiography he describes himself as a 'loner' and says that he was lucky to be rejected for military service because of short-sightedness, because 'my natural inclination to do a left-turn when commanded to do a right might easily have involved me in an uncomfortable conflict' with the drill-sergeant. Intellectually Jespersen's inclination to go his own way expressed itself in scepticism and an urge to contradict, but then it is precisely by argument and counter-argument that progress is made in the scientific pursuit of knowledge.

A striking feature of Jespersen's contribution to scholarship is the enormous amount of it. The sheer size of his output surpasses that of most other researchers with whom it would be natural to compare him. In particular it is the range of his work that surprises, whether within linguistic science generally or in the study of English. Jespersen himself attributed his productivity to the way he would note down thoughts and observations on little slips of paper, which he then arranged according to a flexible decimal system. Jespersen estimated that he had had in all nearly half a million slips, but each time a book was completed he would discard the slips on which it was based. Through my collaboration with Jespersen I saw a lot of these slips, and a thing that struck me as curious was that he himself had cut them with a paper-knife instead of getting a binder or a stationery firm to cut them for him with a guillotine. Each slip was one-eighth of a foolscap sheet, about 10.4 by 8.3 centimetres.

This way of proceeding seemed untypical of Jespersen, who was usually keen to use modern time-saving methods and techniques. He was one of the first scholars to make regular use of a typewriter.

Few scholars of Jespersen's generation – that is, those born around 1860 – have achieved the distinction of being a name that is often quoted to this day in scholarly debate. Again and again one comes upon his name, and not many linguistic works, even among the latest, fail to list one or more of Jespersen's books in their bibliography. The most frequently quoted among his books are undoubtedly *Language*, which was published in 1922, and his great historical grammar, *A Modern English Grammar on Historical Principles*, which runs to seven volumes; the first one was published in 1909 and the last in 1949, that is, after Jespersen's death, when it was prepared by Niels Haislund on the basis of materials and notes left behind by Jespersen.

It can scarcely surprise that, having been published over sixty years ago, his book *Language* is now a little out of date. The surprising thing is that it is still a fascinating and instructive book, which one reads with pleasure. *A Modern English Grammar* is his main work within English studies and perhaps within his output generally. The first volume is one of the few places where Jespersen deals with historical phonology. More source material has since come to light, and on some points his results are in need of correction, but the approach is modern in that he examines the sound system as a whole at successive stages in the history of the language. This enables him to see the changes in a new light. He is the creator of the term 'The Great Vowel Shift', the now generally accepted name for the change by which the spelling of English got out of line with continental languages, so that the letter *a* is now [eɪ] and *e* is [iː]. He also pointed out a parallel in late Middle English to the change in Proto-Germanic known as 'Verner's Law'.

Most of the other volumes of the big grammar deal with syntax. This was a field of study that particularly engaged Jespersen's attention and interest in the last thirty years of his life. According to him, syntax is concerned with the way thought is expressed; it starts from within, from the meaning, and moves towards the form. Jespersen found it increasingly satisfying and pleasurable to concern himself with forms that had a meaning in themselves, instead of with speech sounds in isolation. More and more one perceives the central idea in Jespersen's linguistic philosophy: language is a product of human activity and is consequently the servant of man and not vice versa. The materials in these volumes were arranged in conformity with syntactic theories which Jespersen had evolved over the years, consisting of a system of ranks and two forms of syntactic linking, junction and nexus. These theories have not stood up to later criticism very well, but they have influenced other people's thinking, and regardless of the theoretical point of view the materials in Jespersen's volumes preserve their great value as a splendid collection of examples.

Two more works deserve mention. All anglicists know *Growth and Structure of the English Language* (1905), an engagingly written account of the history of English, characterized by fresh points of view. Another work in the field of English which is seldom mentioned but deserves attention is the indication of pronunciation which Jespersen supplied to Brynildsen's *English and Dano-Norwegian Dictionary* (1902-7).This is probably the first pronouncing dictionary of the century, and it uses a type of notation which in all essentials is identical with that which Daniel Jones was to use later on. The speech that Jespersen recorded was of course that of a generation which has now all but disappeared, the grandparents of present-day Englishmen. This gives the dictionary some historical interest, preceding as it does by quite a few years the first edition of Daniel Jones's dictionary in 1917.

I should like to end by calling attention once more to Jespersen's central idea: the link between sound and sense (*lyd og tyd*, as he put it in Danish, using a word of his own creation); in other words: between language and thought. Quite early on in his youth, in the 1880s, he had argued against the Neo-Grammarians' mechanistic philosophy, according to which sound laws operate blindly like the laws of natural science. To this day there are linguists who hold that to be truly 'scientific' in our study of language we must disregard the fact that human beings are able to think. Unquestionably the study of language becomes infinitely more

10

complicated if we have to consider the speakers' thoughts and feelings and be psychologists as well as philologists, but in the interest of truth we dare not overlook this factor. After all we are humans and not machines, and to Jespersen this was a point of vital significance.

Jørgen Erik Nielsen

OTTO JESPERSEN
AND COPENHAGEN UNIVERSITY

Jens Otto Harry Jespersen was born on 16 July 1860 at Randers in Jutland, but after the death of his father in 1870 the family moved to Hillerød in Northern Zealand, and he was sent to the Frederiksborg grammar school, where he took the university entrance examination in 1877. He chose the language side in school, which meant heavy emphasis on Latin and Greek; in addition, in his spare time he occupied himself with modern languages and from an uncle's library borrowed books in Italian and Spanish.

In September 1877 he took up the study of law at Copenhagen University in accordance with the family tradition: his father, grandfather and great-grandfather had all read law. Besides law, Jespersen had to devote some time to preparing for the Filosofikum, an examination in philosophy obligatory until 1971 for students of all faculties at the end of the freshman year. The course of lectures in that year, 1877-1878, was given by Professor Sophus Heegaard, who dealt in particular with the history of evolutionism from the ancient Greeks to modern times. Harald Høffding, Heegaard's friend and colleague, regards those lectures as probably the zenith of the latter's performance as a university teacher; and Jespersen, who was introduced in this way to the philosophy of Herbert Spencer, expresses his great appreciation of the lectures in his autobiography, and he also mentions them briefly in *Efficiency in Linguistic Change*, p. 5 (Copenhagen, 1941).[1] As a curiosity, Jespersen adds an entirely different reason why Heegaard's lectures were remarkable: women had in that year been admitted to the University for the first time, and among the c.200 freshmen there were two female students!

Jespersen was granted free residence at Regensen, an old hostel

13

steeped in history in the centre of the city, along with a bursary known as 'Kommunitetet', and he was given dinner at the homes of various relatives three days a week. Even so he had to work to keep the wolf from the door, first as a private tutor and later as a shorthand reporter in the Rigsdag (Parliament). In his spare time he cultivated chess, of which he had become fond, and he enjoyed reading French and English literature. Gradually, however, he became tired of studying law, and in the spring of 1881 he made a great decision: he sold his 'law books and bought a second-hand copy of Littré's dictionary and other language books instead'.[2] Thenceforth he was going to devote himself to the study of languages. The importance of speech sounds in language study having become clear to him, Jespersen bought Henry Sweet's *Handbook of Phonetics* (Oxford, 1877), and when the next semester began in September he attended Vilhelm Thomsen's lectures on phonetics, advertised in the University's lecture list for the autumn semester of 1881 as 'an outline of the physiology of speech'. Thomsen, who was then 'Extraordinær Docent' (Reader Extraordinary) of comparative linguistics, becoming Professor in 1887, had over the years 1879 to 1881 lectured on the history of the Romance languages. Jespersen made a copy of these lectures from the notebooks of one of his fellow students, and in the following years he attended Thomsen's lectures on Romance languages as well as on comparative linguistics.

Further, Jespersen attended classes in Old and Modern French given by Thor Sundby, Docent (Reader) in French and from 1887 Professor of Romance philology: the later Professor of English aimed originally at a master's degree in French and other Romance languages. However, Sweet's book prompted him to seek private tuition in English pronunciation from English people living in Copenhagen. Possibly he never availed himself of the conversation classes arranged, according to the lecture list, 'every Wednesday night from 7 to 10' at the home of George Stephens, from 1851 Lektor in English, from 1855 to 1893 Docent but with the title of Professor; but then it seems from *En sprogmands levned* that Jespersen learnt virtually nothing from Stephens. He spread his energies over a vast field; for example, he attended Karl Verner's classes in Russian,[3] and he studied Danish dialects on his own. He had chosen French as his subject owing partly to his linguistic interests, but also because of a predilection for Diderot and other French authors of the 18th century, 'the period when reason (rational thought) had been given pride of place to a greater extent than ever before or later in world history'.[4] Those philosophical interests led him to join a group of students who gathered regularly one evening every month for discussion at Harald Høffding's home.[5]

Otto Jespersen began his prolific activity as a writer in the 1880s, first with a review in *Nordisk Tidsskrift for Filologi*, new series, vol. VI (Copenhagen, 1883-4), of some books on English pronunciation, and then with a Danish translation of Felix Franke's *Die praktische Sprach-erlernung* (Heilbronn, 1884) entitled *Praktisk Tilegnelse af fremmede Sprog* (Copenhagen, 1884). He sent a copy of that book to Vilhelm Thomsen, who thanked him for it in a letter of 9 June 1884 and asked if he would like to write another review for *Nordisk Tidsskrift for Filologi*, this time of Julius Hoffory's *Professor Sievers und die Principien der Sprachpsychologie*.[6] Jespersen complied with Thomsen's request, but he wrote other papers as well, and in 1885 appeared his first original work, *Kortfattet engelsk Grammatik for Tale- og Skriftsproget* (Copenhagen), in which he used phonetic transcription even in his description of syntax. A Swedish translation of that book appeared in Stockholm in 1886: even as a undergraduate Jespersen was making a name for himself as a reformer of the teaching of modern languages.

In 1883 a new university degree, 'Skoleembedseksamen', intended primarily for prospective grammar-school teachers, was instituted alongside the 'Magisterkonferens' (master's degree). The new degree comprised a major subject and two minor ones, Latin being obligatory as one of the minor subjects for students with a modern language or history as major. Jespersen changed over to the new degree, choosing French as his major subject and English as the second minor subject. Like many of the other students, however, he loathed the idea of compulsory Latin, and there being no students' council in those days through which to channel such a complaint, the students chose to invite the professors of the Faculty to a discussion of the issue on 12 November 1884 at Borchs Kollegium, one of the old student hostels in central Copenhagen. Jespersen's invitation to Professor Kristian Erslev, preserved in the manuscript collection of the Royal Library in Copenhagen (NKS 4604-4°), is extended on behalf of 'a considerable number of students'. In *En sprogmands levned* we have Jespersen's description of the meeting (p. 36); the professors stood firm, and Latin remained compulsory until 1901, when a revision of the curricula was carried through. (In the latter year Jespersen as Professor of English was able to influence the decision.) In the summer of 1887 Jespersen passed his finals and at long last got his degree.

A small inheritance, a modest grant from Copenhagen University and a loan from an uncle enabled Jespersen to spend the year 1887-8 abroad: in England, Germany and France. He exchanged some letters with Vilhelm Thomsen, who discussed problems of phonetics with his young friend and tried to advise him about how, when and where to seek financial support, unfortunately without much success! While in Berlin Jespersen received a letter from Thomsen, dated 19 February 1888, which contains the following passage:

> I take this opportunity to make a suggestion. Why don't you concentrate on English language and literature? Before many years have gone by the University will need a new representative of that subject, and at present there is no obvious candidate. Do consider whether that might not be an opening for you. Could you not write, say, a dissertation on some English subject (preferably not a purely phonetic one)?[7]

The words within brackets reveal that phonetics was not in those days regarded as a worthy branch of learning among Thomsen's colleagues at Copenhagen University. For Jespersen the letter became decisive: in his reply written from 'Neuilly près Paris 13/3/88' he thanked Thomsen for his advice, to which he was giving careful consideration, having almost made up his mind to return to Berlin for the summer term of 1888 to attend Professor Zupitza's seminars in the Department of English. He carried out this plan and returned to Copenhagen in August. There he resumed work as a teacher, but in addition to his other commitments found time to write the book *Studier over engelske kasus*, which he defended for the doctorate on 12 May 1891, the appointed examiners ('opponents') being George Stephens and Hermann Møller, Professor of Germanic philology, while Vilhelm Thomsen and Harald Høffding acted as unofficial 'opponents'.[8]

A doctor's degree entitles the holder to teach in the University as an unpaid 'Privatdocent'. This Jespersen did in the following semesters, holding classes in Old English and Chaucer and thus acquiring additional qualifications for a university post. The opening came in 1893, when George Stephens handed in his resignation. In a letter dated 13 January 1893 Vilhelm Thomsen thanks Jespersen for having sent him a copy of the recently published *Chaucers liv og digtning*, practically Jespersen's only work on English literature, which he wrote to demonstrate that he had paid attention to the literary side of the subject as well. Thomsen's letter contains this piece of information of interest to his friend: 'At the Faculty meeting yesterday it was merely decided to recommend to the Ministry that the post should be advertised as vacant'. The Ministry did this, and in that same spring changed the post from a Docentship to a Professorship of English Language and Literature.

There were four applicants: William A. Craigie, Dr. Adolf Hansen, Dr. Otto Jespersen and Dr. Jón Stefánsson. Craigie, the later lexicographer, was then a very young man, and the Faculty in its report emphasised that so far he had not produced any work of scholarship; Hansen was an able though not a distinguished scholar, but he did not master the linguistic side of the subject; Stefánsson had written little besides his dissertation; moreover, his scholarly method had met with serious and well documented criticism, and his reaction to that criticism had not been commendable. For those reasons the Faculty could not recommend the appointment of any of those three applicants for the chair of English. Jespersen, on the other hand, was very well qualified: he spoke English perfectly, was fully conversant with modern philology and was also familiar with English literature. The Faculty's recommendation was approved by the Konsistorium, the supreme governing body of the University, and sent on to the Ministry, and Jespersen was appointed under the Royal Seal as from 1 May 1893.[9]

Being barely 33, Jespersen was younger than the majority of the professors in the Faculty of Arts, some of whom have already been mentioned. Among colleagues roughly his own age we may name Kristoffer Nyrop (from 1888, Romance Languages), Verner Dahlerup (from 1899, Nordic Languages), Holger Pedersen (from 1900, Slavonic Languages and Comparative Linguistics) and Christian Sarauw (from 1908, German), in collaboration with whom Jespersen wrote his English primer entitled *Engelsk Begynderbog*. (1895).[10]

In May 1893 Adolf Hansen, who had for many semesters been a 'Privatdocent' as well as an external examiner at Copenhagen University, applied to the Ministry for appointment as a regular Docent; the University recommended his employment in this capacity pointing to the fact that English is a comprehensive subject which is also of interest to students of other subjects. As a result the University was granted permission to employ Adolf Hansen as from 1 April 1894 to 'give lectures and conduct seminars on English language and literature'. From then on English had two regular teachers, something which Romance languages had had since 1888, but which German got only in 1908. Unlike Jespersen, Adolf Hansen specialised in literature, and in his capacity as Docent taught literature besides proficiency in written English, i.e. translation from Danish. Jespersen was responsible for the other linguistic aspects of English, but he also took the students through works of literature, giving introductory lectures followed by a reading of the work in question with the emphasis on the students' correct understanding of the text. But, as he put it himself (*En sprogmands levned*, p. 124), he rarely engaged in 'aestheticism and evaluation'. David Grünbaum, one of his students, later described him as 'dry, indeed almost shy' even when they were doing Shelley (Jespersen's favourite poet) or Keats, and Grünbaum attributes this to 'a certain type of spiritual modesty' (David Grünbaum,

18

Som dagene gik (Copenhagen, 1970), p. 55).

Adolf Hansen died in 1908, and as his successor the University appointed Dr. Vilhelm Grønbech, who had lectured as a 'Privatdocent' for a couple of semesters on various subjects including English literature. In its recommendation to the Ministry concerning his appointment the Faculty emphasised the importance of English at the university level: the new Education Act of 1903 ('Loven af 1903 om højere Almenskoler') made heavier demands on grammar-school teachers and had caused an increased intake of new students. The person who was needed must be capable of teaching English literature and the history of English civilization, and this, as well as phonetic transcription, is what Grønbech taught after his appointment. In 1911, however, he took over a chair of the History of Religion, and Dr. Niels Bøgholm was appointed as his successor; like Grønbech he was an old student of Jespersen's, but unlike his predecessor Bøgholm was primarily a linguist.

The increasing number of students of English caused the Faculty to apply to the Ministry of Education in 1914 for permission to have Jes Skovgaard appointed as an extra Docent in English. As a result Skovgaard was appointed from 1 April 1916, but he resigned after only four years, and the person appointed to succeed him in 1921 was Aage Brusendorff, who like Skovgaard was primarily interested in literature, and who later became Jespersen's successor as Professor. Bøgholm's post had in 1919 been changed into a Professorship, so in Jespersen's last years at the University there were two professors of English and one Docent. The men just named were specialists within different fields of the subject, but no sharp distinction was made between language and literature; in general, language was more conspicuously represented than literature. In *En sprogmands levned* (pp. 150-51) Jespersen mentions an instance of an English-speaking scholar giving lectures in the University: Professor W. H. Schofield from Harvard lectured on 'Chivalry in English literature' in the spring of 1911. Jespersen used this visit as a good opportunity to explain to the public, in an article ('Videnskabens kår') in the Copenhagen daily *Politiken* on 13 May 1911, the straitened circumstances of scholars and scientists in Denmark. Professor Schofield, he said, is at the moment the guest of Copenhagen University, but in reality *he* is the host, because unfortunately the university has no funds to defray his expenses. Jespersen also complains that the seminar libraries are not housed in a suitable building, that professors' salaries are low, and that no limit prevents professors from continuing to hold their chairs into extreme old age. Jespersen himself, to be on the safe side, has exacted from his wife a solemn vow that she is to shoot him if he does not resign when he is 65!

On 13 April 1897 Otto Jespersen had married Ane Marie Djørup, and the Jespersens lived in Copenhagen, at 15 Carl Bernhards Vej in the borough of Frederiksberg, till 1901, when with their son they moved to Jægersborg near Gentofte, north of the city, where they rented and later bought a house named Ermelundsly. This was their home until 1934, when they moved to Lundehave, a grand house on the north-western outskirts of Elsinore donated by a benefactor to the Royal Danish Academy of Sciences and Letters for use as a grace-and-favour residence for a distinguished scientist or scholar. Jespersen was the first occupant of the house in that capacity.

Ermelundsly was situated about 20 minutes' walk from Gentofte station, from where another 20 minutes by train took Jespersen to Copenhagen. In *En sprogmands levned* (p. 188) Jespersen regrets that the professors had moved away from the centre, which made intercourse with other professors and with students difficult. (In those days scarcely any professor of an Arts subject had a room in the University.) Still, he had colleagues living in the vicinity, e.g. Vilhelm Grønbech, Kristoffer Nyrop and Kristian Sandfeld, and the students too found their way to Ermelundsly, where the Jespersens kept open house on the first Sunday of each month during the semesters.

Jespersen did most of his reading and writing at home, and he obviously enjoyed that; indeed he thought it possible that his book *Sprogundervisning* (1901) had received its special tone from having to a large extent been written in the garden of Ermelundsly. In August 1914 he removed his most valuable scholarly notes to a farmhouse, as Ermelundsly stood near the line of defence built by the Danish Army, and

20

might have to be demolished if Denmark was attacked. For some weeks
the house, situated near an important bridge and housing a telephone,
had soldiers billeted, but fortunately Denmark was not drawn into that
war. The country was less fortunate during the Second World War, and
during the winters of the German occupation 'Lundehave became a grim
place with a forbidding view of the frozen Sound'. However, C.A.
Bodelsen, to whom we are indebted for that description, also recalls the
pleasant aspects of Jespersen's homes: from Lundehave he mentions how
'his study commanded a view like that from the bridge of a ship'; and he
recollects talks with Jespersen at Ermelundsly 'in his high-ceilinged
study, where the green light filtering through the ivy fell on his revolving
bookcase with the Oxford Dictionary, and on his desk with the bundles
of slips and the typewriter'.[11]

In such surroundings Jespersen did his scholarly work; in fact the
names of those two places frequently appear at the bottom of his prefaces; and there he entertained visitors.[12] His teaching was given in the
old university buildings in the centre of the city, to which his adminis-
trative duties also called him. He was Dean of the Faculty of Arts from
November 1904 to November 1906 and Rektor (Vice-Chancellor) of the
University from November 1920 to November 1921, so it was his privi-
lege to deliver the address of welcome at the inauguration on 3 March
1921 of the Institute for Theoretical Physics in Copenhagen (since 1965
called the Niels Bohr Institute).[13] Jespersen himself mentions another
memorable event during that year, the 50th anniversary of Georg Brandes' first lectures on 'Main Currents of Nineteenth-Century Literature' in
1871, which the University commemorated by inviting Brandes to deliver a series of lectures in the Great Hall; for his subject Brandes chose
The Odyssey.[14] Jespersen was an old admirer of Brandes and in 1897
had been one of the supporters in the Faculty of a proposal to create a
chair for Brandes, who for political reasons had not been appointed to
the chair of literature in 1872. The scheme did not succeed, but in 1902
the new Liberal government granted the old 'aristocratic radical' a professor's salary.

Two of the speeches delivered by Jespersen in his capacity as

Jørgen Erik Nielsen

Rektor have been printed in his book *Tanker og studier* (Copenhagen, 1932), pp. 18-26 and 61-80 respectively. The first is his speech of welcome to the freshmen on 3 September 1921, in which he exhorts the new students to absorb the scholarly and scientific tradition (to the extent of being critical of their professors!), the only genuine hallmark of academics. The other speech, which he called 'Sproglige værdier' ('Linguistic Values'), is one that he delivered at the annual celebration ('årsfest') of the University on 17 November 1921. It is full of interesting, illuminating examples, with the emphasis on language as 'consisting of human acts', in short, a typical Otto Jespersen lecture. In 1922, the year following Jespersen's Rektorship, he was in Italy with Mrs Jespersen celebrating their silver wedding, and together with Professor Biilmann, his successor as Rektor, he represented Denmark at the 700th anniversary of the University of Padua.

Jespersen took an active interest in the life of his University, and in 1914 he formulated his wishes for it in an article ('Universitetsønsker') in the periodical *Tilskueren* (Copenhagen), pp. 124-33. That article, longer and more detailed than the one in *Politiken* in 1911 (see p. 19), is both sharp and provocative, and it is not surprising that some of his fellow professors did not like it. Thus he argues that there ought not to be a Faculty of Divinity in a modern university; he held that Copenhagen University should have many more chairs; that the country needed more than one university; that the University administration worked too slowly and was being impeded by too many old professors on the governing bodies; that besides the Rektor there ought to be a University Administrator; that the lack of scholarships and the salary system for young graduates created no incentives for young people to go on to postgraduate studies; and that exams consumed too much time and energy. The existence of only one university (Aarhus University did not open till 1928) led easily, he thought, to ossification, but he saw the establishment since 1911 of a students' council as a healthy counter-measure enabling the students to bring a beneficial influence to bear. Another step forward, he thought, had been achieved by the establishment of the seminar libraries in 1896, though he found their budget disgracefully small. In *En sprogmands levned*, pp. 153-4 and 187-9, Jespersen recurred to his article of many years before and his other wishes for change in the University and could then note with satisfaction that the intervening years had seen many improvements, in some of which he had had a share.

In this connection we should not forget the revisions of the curriculum for the 'Skoleembedseksamen' in 1901 and in 1924. After 1901 Latin was no longer compulsory as one of the two minor subjects; another change was that it became obligatory for major-subject students of English to offer a specified number of pages by Chaucer; it seems easy to see Jespersen's hand in those two alterations. The 1924 revision made reading of Spenser and Milton compulsory: the Jespersen who had been in favour of abolishing Latin would have been applauded by the student revolutionaries around 1970, but the Jespersen who created three sacred cows (Chaucer, Spenser and Milton) to join Shakespeare, who had been one since 1883, would have been booed. In 1926 the Faculty decided that some knowledge of Latin was to be obligatory for all its students, with the exception of psychologists, and students who had not done Latin in school would have to attend a course and pass an examination in the subject. Louis L. Hammerich informs us in *Duo* (Copenhagen, 1973), p. 408, that as a young professor of German in the early 1920s he had discussed the desirability of such a measure with Christian Sarauw, who advised him to wait until Otto Jespersen had retired. For students of English the rule was operative until 1974, when the Study Board for English ('Engelsk Studienævn') abolished it; Jespersen must certainly have nodded approvingly in his Elysium.

As one more instance of beneficial change in the University Jespersen mentions in *En sprogmands levned* the decision of 1920 that doctoral dissertations need no longer be in Danish. This meant that a Copenhagen dissertation became more easily part and parcel of current international scholarship. That rule prompted Aage Brusendorff to translate and thoroughly revise his thesis on Chaucer, which he then defended in 1925, when Jespersen was an official examiner for the last time. Naturally he had acted in that capacity many times before, and according to L.L. Hammerich he could be severe (*Duo*, p. 415).

At the beginning of the autumn term of 1924 Otto Jespersen announced to his students that he had decided to retire after another year: at the age of 65 one ought to give place to younger men, he said, and he wanted to devote all his time to various scholarly work in progress. Jespersen was the first professor to avail himself of the recently introduced right to retire at the age of 65; in fact, the Civil Servants Act ('Tjenestemandsloven') of 12 September 1919 obliged civil servants to retire at 70, and thus another of Jespersen's great ideas had been realized. In *En sprogmands levned* (p. 189) he says that he was afraid that advancing years might begin to tell; and judging from the recollections of a couple of students from his last years, there is some reason to think that his teaching had become rather too much a matter of routine. At his best he had taught his students to pay careful attention to linguistic details and to aim at clarity in their explanations. He was exacting as a teacher, but also kind and helpful to his students, many of whom cherished happy memories both of the Professor in the lecture-room and of visits to his home.[15] The many journeys he undertook could not all take place in his holidays, so a couple of times he had to apply for exemption from his teaching duties, for example in the autumn semesters of 1904 and 1909, which he spent in the USA. In the autumn of 1913 he introduced the students to his interest in auxiliary languages by giving a course of nine lectures on Ido followed by a tenth lecture *in* Ido, which the students translated sentence by sentence.[16]

On 25 May 1925 Jespersen delivered his farewell lecture in the University's main building, Room 6. In this lecture, printed in *Tanker og studier*, pp. 7-17, and in an English translation in his *Linguistica* (Copenhagen, 1933), pp. 1-11, he reviews his life, arguing that his undogmatic approach to linguistic problems had been his reaction to the uninspired rote learning of his days as a student of law. He also mentions the decisive letter from Vilhelm Thomsen, but gives the impression that he received it in England, an error which he corrects in *En sprogmands levned*, p. 57. Many colleagues, students and friends attended the lecture; the students presented Jespersen with a vase, and the Dean, Professor Vilhelm Grønbech, thanked the retiring Professor on behalf of the Faculty of Arts.[17]

Otto Jespersen had a long and happy retirement, in which he continued his scholarly work, witness *A Modern English Grammar* and *Novial Lexike,*to name only two examples.[18] He continued to go abroad, sometimes to attend conferences, and he was president of the 1936 Congress of Linguists in Copenhagen, on which occasion the delegates paid a visit to the Jespersens at Lundehave. A couple of times he acted as unofficial examiner at the public defence of a thesis, and he continued to attend meetings of the Royal Danish Academy of Sciences and Letters, of which he had been a member since 21 April 1899. The death on 30 March 1937 of Ane Marie Jespersen marked the end of a very happy marriage and left him a lonely man, and the outbreak of another World War, which led to the German occupation of Denmark on 9 April 1940, caused him great disappointment and anxiety besides the inconveniences brought about by fuel and traffic restrictions. In those winters he felt very isolated in his large house, which could only be partially heated. But he was never forgotten: on his 80th birthday on 16 July 1940 he was presented with the book *Hilsen til Otto Jespersen på firs-aarsdagen 16. juli 1940* (Copenhagen, 1940), in which a great number of old students, colleagues and friends have written about their impressions of him.

In December 1942 he went to Roskilde in spite of illness to spend Christmas with his son and daughter-in-law. His condition worsened after Christmas, and he had to go to hospital with a bladder complaint, was given a couple of operations, appeared to be recovering and resumed work, for example dictating to Niels Haislund, his secretary, the preface to *A Modern English Grammar*, vol. VII. However, fever returned, and he passed away on 30 April 1943. His body was taken to Lundehave, where on 4 May a funeral service took place in the presence of both his family and university friends and colleagues, among them Niels Bohr (who was shortly afterwards to flee from occupied Denmark and spend some years in the USA), L.L. Hammerich and C.A. Bodelsen, who was Jespersen's successor at one remove. William Thalbitzer, Professor of Eskimo Language, spoke of Jespersen's impact on the study of languages, and Vilhelm Andersen, Emeritus Professor of Danish Literature, spoke of Jespersen as an old friend. The graveside ceremony was performed by the Rev. Karl Jespersen, a nephew of the deceased, and then the coffin was taken to Elsinore for cremation. A few days later the urn was interred in the cemetery at Elsinore beside that of Mrs Jespersen.[19]

Otto Jespersen's last resting-place is in a seaport which has age-old links with that wider world of which he was a citizen, but it is also within easy walking distance of a house, a garden and a countryside which he loved and where he spent the last years of a long and busy life.

Notes

1. Harald Høffding, *Erindringer* (Copenhagen, 1928), pp. 103-4; Otto Jespersen, *En sprogmands levned* (Copenhagen, 1938), pp. 22-3; see Hans Frede Nielsen's article in the present volume, p. 69.

2. Otto Jespersen, *En sprogmands levned*, p. 28. All quotations from Danish have been translated by the present writer.

3. See Jespersen's obituary article 'Karl Verner', originally in *Tilskueren* (Copenhagen), Jan. 1897, pp. 3-18, reprinted in his *Tanker og studier* (Copenhagen, 1932), pp. 32-47, and in an English translation in his *Linguistica. Selected Papers in English, French and German* (Copenhagen, 1933), pp. 12-23.

4. *En sprogmands levned*, p. 33.

5. Høffding describes those evenings in his *Erindringer*, pp. 121-6; like Jespersen he expresses himself warmly about them, though with a touch of bitterness against one of the then young students, the later poet Johannes Jørgensen, who mentions the evenings at Høffding's in his *Mit Livs Legende*, vol. I: *Den røde Stjærne* (Copenhagen, 1916), pp. 146-8. Jørgensen does not disparage them, but as a newly converted Roman Catholic he felt he had to dis-

sociate himself throughout his autobiography from his own youth. Valdemar Vedel, in an article ('Studenterminder fra 1880erne') printed in his book *Firsernes førere* (Copenhagen, 1923), pp. 7-10, devotes four pages to the evenings with Høffding.

6. The letters quoted in this article are all preserved in the Royal Library in Copenhagen: Thomsen's letters to Jespersen under the call number NKS, 3975 – 4°, Jespersen's to Thomsen under the call number NKS, 4291 – 4°. The Danish linguist Hoffory was until 1889 a professor in Berlin, where Jespersen saw a good deal of him during his stays there.

7. Jespersen quotes those lines in *En sprogmands levned*, p. 57, changing Thomsen's spelling of 'koncentrere' to 'konsentrere'. In his autobiography *Livsdagen lang* (Copenhagen, 1947), p. 39, Louis Bobé asserts that to Stephens atheism and phonetics were equally detestable intellectual movements.

8. *En sprogmands levned*, p. 69 and Hans Frede Nielsen's article in the present volume, p. 71.

9. The Faculty's recommendation, like all similar information, is accessible in *Aarbog for Københavns Universitet*, the University's yearbook. In *Nordisk Tidsskrift for Filologi*, 3rd series, vol. I (Copenhagen 1892-3) Stefánsson had been proved by Jespersen to have used plagiarism in his thesis *Robert Browning* (Copenhagen, 1891), and this had led to a bitter controversy; see *En sprogmands levned*, pp. 72-3.

10. See Paul Christophersen's article in the present volume, p. 1; some earlier books are mentioned in Knud Sørensen's article in the present volume, pp. 34-8.

11. C.A. Bodelsen, 'Otto Jespersen' in his *Essays and Papers* (Copenhagen, 1964), pp. 179-93; the lines quoted are on p. 192.

12. A description of a visit to Ermelundsly in the days of Jespersen's retirement is found in Haruko Ichikawa (Mrs. Sanki Ichikawa), *Japanese Lady in Europe* (London, 1937), pp. 258-61.

13. Peter Robertson, *The Early Years: The Niels Bohr Institute 1921-1930* (Copenhagen, 1979), pp. 38-40.

14. *En sprogmands levned*, p. 179. Svend Norrild, who attended those lectures as a student, mentions them in his *Dansk Litteratur fra Saxo til Kaj Munk*, vol. II (Copenhagen, 1949), pp. 71-2.

15. My main source of information about Jespersen as a teacher is the book *Hilsen til Otto Jespersen på firs-aarsdagen 16. juli 1940* (Copenhagen, 1940); in books of that type one naturally does not find many remarks of a critical nature.

16. *En sprogmands levned*, p. 135; C.A. Bodelsen, *Essays and Papers*, p. 191; those lectures are not mentioned in the University's lecture list, but the final lecture ('Finala diskurso') is printed in *Progreso* (Paris), No. 73, 1914.

17. The event is described in great detail in the Copenhagen daily *Berlingske Tidende*, 26 May 1925.

18. Bibliographies of Jespersen's works are found in *A Grammatical Miscellany Offered to Otto Jespersen on His 70th Birthday* (Copenhagen, 1930), pp. 433-57 and in *Det Kgl. danske Videnskabernes Selskab. Oversigt over Selskabets Virksomhed Juni 1943 – Maj 1944* (Copenhagen, 1944), pp. 57-63.

19. The information about Jespersen's final illness and death is taken from the two Copenhagen dailies *Berlingske Tidende* and *Politiken*, 1 and 5 Maj 1943.

Knud Sørensen

THE TEACHING OF ENGLISH IN DENMARK AND OTTO JESPERSEN

There have been cultural contacts between England and Denmark for more than a thousand years, but during most of this period the knowledge of the English language among Danes was extremely limited. A beginning interest in English may be noted from the last quarter of the seventeenth century, which saw the publication of three books intended as aids for the study of English: F. Bolling's *Fuldkommen Engelske Grammatica*, which also contained the first English-Danish dictionary (Copenhagen, 1678); H.T. Gerner's *Orthographia Danica*, which included a brief guide to the pronunciation of English (Copenhagen, 1679); and C.L. Nyborg's *Addresse til Det Engelske Sprogs Læszning*, which was in the nature of a phrase-book with information concerning pronunciation and grammar (Copenhagen, 1698).[1]

However, in the eighteenth century and the greater part of the nineteenth the dominant foreign languages in Denmark were Greek, Latin, German, and French; down to the mid-eighteenth century very little was known in Denmark about English language and literature, and there was as yet no institutionalized teaching of the subject. But about 1750 English literature began to attract the attention of cultured Danes, who became familiar with Shakespeare, the Spectator essays, the Ossianic poems, and the classical school of poetry. These works were read in translation, but it may be noted that the first translations were done from German into Danish, not direct from English.[2]

The gradual discovery of English literature went hand in hand with a growing realization that English was a language of commercial importance. A need accordingly came to be felt for aids for the study of English, and the first to publish a reasonably adequate English grammar

29

in Denmark, *Rudimenta Grammaticæ anglicanæ* (1750), was the Englishman Charles Bertram. In his dedication to King Frederik V he gives as his reason for publishing the book that it may prove useful for students and sailors and for people who trade with Great Britain. In the preface an anonymous poetaster eulogizes Bertram in characteristic eighteenth-century fashion, at the same time providing an apposite comment on the position of English in Denmark at the time:

> ...
> Now to this Treasure [i.e. the English language]
> never heretofore
> Could any Dane in Danish find a Door
> But either must by French or German Clew,
> With weary Strides pass *uncouth Lab'rynths* thro':
> Or else give o'er, and sighingly complain:
> That there's no Means at Home their Wish to gain!
> Thus for a Grammar in their Tongue they cry'd
> Full long in Vain; 'till BERTRAM he comply'd
> With their Entreaties, and thro' many a *Maze*,
> With Skilfull Pen, the *English Tongue* did trace, ...

Bertram stressed the commercial usefulness of a knowledge of English, and so did the Norwegian Andreas Berthelson, compiler of an English-Danish dictionary,[3] who observed in his preface: 'I have particularly concentrated on those words and locutions that are indispensable to merchants and sailors'.

The realization that English was a useful language had other consequences: the 1780s saw the foundation of two schools in Copenhagen, Borgerdydskolen and Efterslægtselskabets Skole, which unlike the existing grammar schools were to cater for boys who wanted to go in for a commercial career. In these new schools Latin and Greek were therefore largely crowded out by the modern languages, and English was taught there although it took third place after German and French.

If we go on to consider the external conditions governing the teaching of English in nineteenth-century Denmark, we note that during this period there was a growing tendency for the modern languages to be strengthened at the expense of the classical languages; but it was only rather late in the century that English acquired a position of some prominence in the educational system. As a Scandinavian philologist put it in 1837: it was long before Danish was accepted as a worthy grammar-school subject; among the other modern languages French and German were chosen, no doubt because the literatures of those languages were widely read; English was also thought of, but no teaching of this language was carried into effect.[4] Practically everywhere English was optional as a school subject. It *was* taught in a few grammar schools, but this usually depended on whether the school in question had available a qualified teacher. The School Act of 1871 introduced a division into a language side and a mathematics side, and in the former, English was now made obligatory. The School Act of 1903 considerably strengthened the position of German and English at the expense of French, Latin, and Greek. English was now taught in some of the teacher training colleges, but it was only in 1930 that it became a compulsory subject there.

The crying lack of qualified teachers was due to the fact that English was only slowly gaining recognition as an academic subject. The first to be given the title of Professor of English Language and Literature at the University of Copenhagen was T.C. Bruun (1750-1834), who from 1802 until his death trained students in conversation and composition and lectured on the English classics. But as yet English could not be said to have become a subject that rested on a sound scholarly foundation. The post was vacant at the University from 1834 to 1851, when the Englishman George Stephens (1813-95) was appointed lecturer in English; he was a 'docent' from 1855 to 1893. His real interest was runology, and judging from Otto Jespersen's autobiography[5] he was very inefficient as a teacher. It was not till after Jespersen had been appointed to the first 'ordinary' Chair of English in 1893 that it became possible to study English on a sound scholarly basis.[6] The introduction of an M.A. degree qualifying the holder for teaching in secondary schools involved an appreciable raising of the level of modern foreign language teaching.

To return to the way English was taught before Jespersen. If one examines textbooks[7] and studies the pedagogical debate of the time, it is possible to form a fairly clear impression of the methods used.

In general there was a very imperfect realization of the fact that every language has its own autonomous structure and that the modern languages studied differed structurally from Greek or Latin. Grammatical description tended to be rather heavily latinized – the approach that Jespersen was to term 'squinting grammar'. English was not accounted for in terms of English structure, but was forced into Latin moulds. Thus, in a grammar from the latter half of the eighteenth century the reader is presented with the following paradigm:

Nom.	the King
Gen.	of the King, or the King's
Dat.	to the King
Acc.	the King
Voc.	O King
Abl.	from the King[8]

The drilling of rules was emphasized, while the pupil's own observation of the foreign language was neglected. Sometimes the grammars were stamped by a peculiar archaism in the forms prescribed. This is true of a book from 1837, S. Rosing's *Kortfattet Engelsk Sproglære til Skolebrug* ('Brief English Grammar for the Use of Schools'), which lists forms like *thou turnest – thou turnedst*, so that the user must have received a warped impression of contemporary English. Perhaps this grammatical archaism was due to the fact that the textbooks did not normally offer contemporary English literature, but specimens of older classical texts.

As for the acquisition of vocabulary, rote-learning appears to have been a favourite method (indeed it was to some extent continued down to the writer's own schooldays in the early forties). About 1830, we are told, the students at the Naval Academy in Copenhagen were supposed to memorize a total of 12,000 words in English and French.[9] In the light of this it is hardly surprising that the translation exercises which loomed so large in the teaching of foreign languages were often done on the basis of sentences that were devoid of any sort of natural context.

The written language was given pride of place at the expense of the spoken language. A major reason for this is probably the fact that there were not many teachers who had an adequate command of natural spoken English,[10] and that the knowledge of phonetics was very poor. In his autobiography Jespersen reports how a headmaster asserted that Danish pupils could not possibly be taught to pronounce the voiced *s* found in French and English.[11] But even if all this is taken into consideration, it is difficult to understand today why it was with such downright fanaticism that many language-teachers were opposed to letting their pupils speak the foreign language. Towards the close of the nineteenth century a language-teacher voiced his objection as follows:

> ... occasionally – and I imagine that this is done almost exclusively in girls' schools – the practice is resorted to of 'speaking the language in class', nobody considering how useless this is or indeed how much damage it can do ...; if, once in a while, the teacher succeeds in starting a pupil talking, the only result is that this pupil will be moving across the treacherous swamp of guesswork with a certain measure of breeziness or even downright audacity, and this is nothing if not demoralizing, since it is bound to lead to an incessant obliteration of the limits between what the pupil knows and what he is ignorant of.[12]

This statement represents the general view of the time. It may be added, however, that there was at least one nineteenth-century teacher of English, Carl Mariboe (1800-1860), who was to some extent a forerunner of Jespersen. Mariboe introduced James Hamilton's method of language-teaching, which was based on two principles: the language should be presented to the pupils as a living organism, and its laws should be learned from their own observation, not through the inculcation of rules.

In another respect, though, Mariboe's teaching method differed from Jespersen's: he believed in the usefulness of verbatim, i.e. often unidiomatic, translation.[13]

To sum up it may be said that until the end of the nineteenth century the teaching of English was dominated by squinting grammar, formalism, rote-learning, a strong emphasis on translation, and a concentration on printed texts, so that in effect the methods employed in the teaching of modern foreign languages were largely identical with those used in the teaching of the dead classical languages.

It was this state of things that Otto Jespersen reacted vigorously against when he joined the pedagogical debate in the 1880s. He became the leading Danish exponent of radical new approaches in the teaching of modern languages, particularly English and French; but he had of course received inspiration from predecessors in the field.

We do not know whether Jespersen knew Jan Amos Comenius (1592-1670), some of whose views on language teaching he would undoubtedly have subscribed to; for instance, according to Comenius a language should be taught rather through use and practice than through the drilling of grammatical rules; the teaching of isolated words is useless; words should be associated with the 'things' to which they refer (for instance objects like chairs and tables in the classroom); and for such objects as are not present, pictures and drawings may be resorted to.[14] We do know, however, that the views of N.M. Petersen (1791-1862) were known to Jespersen, for he quotes him with approval; according to N.M. Petersen the natural way of learning a language is by practising it (in the same way as one learns one's native language), and it is pointless to teach rules and paradigms to the pupils.[15]

Jespersen explicitly acknowledges his indebtedness to a number of other people as well: the Norwegian Johan Storm, whose *Engelsk Filologi, I. Det levende Sprog*, had appeared in 1879, stressing the importance of spoken English; Henry Sweet, whose books *A Handbook of Phonetics* (1877) and *Elementarbuch des gesprochenen Englisch* (1885) appealed strongly to him; and the German scholar Wilhelm Viëtor, who in 1882 published his pamphlet *Der Sprachunterricht muss umkehren!* Further, it is important to refer to Jespersen's connection with the young German Felix Franke. In 1884 Jespersen became acquainted with Franke's booklet, entitled *Die praktische Spracherlernung auf Grund der Psychologie und Physiologie der Sprache dargestellt.*[16] Jespersen felt that here was a kindred spirit whose views on language learning and teaching tallied with his own, so he wrote to the author and asked his permission to translate the booklet into Danish. Permission was readily granted, and the same year saw the publication of *Praktisk Tilegnelse af fremmede Sprog*, adapted by Otto Jespersen, who added a motto by Johan Storm: 'Sproget må læres således, som det forekommer i det virkelige Liv' ('Language should be learnt in the same way as it appears in real life'). Other kindred spirits were the Swede J.A. Lundell and the Norwegian August Western, two people whom Jespersen met at the third conference of Scandinavian philologists, held at Stockholm in 1886, and with whom he formed a Scandinavian association, *Quousque Tandem*, whose purpose was to advocate the principles that ought to govern a reformed way of teaching modern foreign languages.[17] These principles were expounded by Jespersen in an article that he published in 1886[18] and later, in greater detail, in his book *Sprogundervisning* (1901).[19] They concern the following points:

(1) It is the spoken language, not the written language, that should form the basis of teaching. An essential aim of language-teaching should be to make the pupils realize that they are working with a living language, and hence to equip them with a fair oral proficiency, including of course the ability to understand the foreign language as used by native speakers. It cannot be doubted that reform was sorely needed here. Up till the time when the reform movement got under way, the grammar – translation method had been the dominant one, the result being a poor standard of pronunciation and little if any oral proficiency. This was bound up with the fact that most teachers were poor models to their pupils as far as the spoken language was concerned. As to pronunciation, it is relevant to point out that phonetics had made great strides in the latter half of the nineteenth century, and that Jespersen and the other reformers were able and keen phoneticians. Jespersen strongly advocates

the exclusive use of phonetic transcription during the early stages of language-teaching, and he emphasizes that the transcription system employed should be precise and unambiguous. The principle of transcription was not unknown, but the systems then in use were often more of a hindrance than a help: they were confined to the normal letters of the alphabet which were used inconsistently in ways that were sometimes clearly influenced by spelling or by the Danish sound system.[20]

(2) As far as is at all possible, use should be made of coherent texts with a sensible content, right from the beginning of teaching. This principle was urged as a reaction against the use in primers of isolated, disconnected, sometimes even nonsensical sentences selected or made up in such a way as to illustrate a grammatical point. Further, Jespersen advocated a reasonable selection of a not too extensive vocabulary, based on frequency and adapted to the pupils' understanding. The two points are connected and also tie up with (3) below. To illustrate the use of disconnected sentences I subjoin a brief specimen:

> 56. Who can have put that into his head? 57. Many people lead a gay life whether they can afford it or not. 58. Did you ring, ma'am? 59. Her heart was not so easily won as he imagined. 60. I will write it down at once, that I may not forget it.[21]

As against this, Jespersen makes the point that it is extremely important to get especially young learners to take an interest in what they are reading, and he adds that textbook writers should be concerned to include self-interpreting sentences in which the meaning of a word may be deduced from the context.

(3) Grammatical observation should be practised in close connection with the study of texts and at the initial stage should be limited to an absolute minimum. Jespersen is strongly critical of the rote-learning of rigmaroles and rules that are often not understood, and he quotes with approval Herbert Spencer's reference to 'that intensely stupid custom, the

teaching of grammar to children'.[22] Instead, he makes a plea for what may be termed 'inventional grammar': the pupils should be stimulated to go treasure-hunting in the text for examples on the basis of which they can make up their own grammatical rules. They should never be told by the teacher what they can find out for themselves. The text can also be used as a basis for transformational exercises of various kinds, for example turning verbs in the present tense into past-tense forms.

At later stages of the language-learning process Jespersen is not against systematic grammar, which may be used as an aid in formulating precisely a rule that the intermediate learner has acquired a vague idea about through his reading – in other words the inductive approach being supported by deduction. But he is against pedantically attaching importance to grammatical oddities, and he also criticizes the systematic approach of many grammatical treatments. For instance, morphology and syntax should not be divorced; form and function should be taught simultaneously. Therefore he objects to the listing in the same paradigm of the forms *my* and *mine*; for their different functions are syntactically determined.

(4) The final point concerns the role of translation in language-teaching, which in Jespersen's view is far too dominant. He does not absolutely rule out translation, but he urges that it should be severely limited, and that other exercises should be used instead to make the learners understand the text. One possibility is to give explanations in the foreign language so as to establish in the pupils' minds an association between words and sentences and the things and concepts they refer to. Another useful exercise consists in the pupils retelling in their own words the text they have read.

Translation is, however, an ambiguous term. Jespersen emphasizes that a distinction should be made between translation into one's native language and translation into the foreign language. The former may be used to a limited extent simply as a practical means to test whether the pupil has understood the text, while translation into the foreign language 'is, for beginners at least, an extremely poor means in comparison with the many other hitherto generally neglected ways in which the teacher

Knud Sørensen

may get a pupil to say (or write) something in the foreign language'.[23]

The points discussed above represent the programme of the new – or 'direct' – method of foreign-language teaching, which Jespersen frequently advocated in the pedagogical debate among secondary-school teachers. He also quickly proceeded to embody these principles in a set of school textbooks. His first book, published in 1885, has the significant title *Kortfattet Engelsk Grammatik for Tale- og Skriftsproget* ('Brief English Grammar of the Spoken and Written Language'), in which spoken English (in phonetic transcription) was given a prominent position. The year 1889 saw the publication of his *Fransk Læsebog efter Lydskriftsmetoden* ('French Primer in Accordance with the Transcription Method'), and in 1895 Jespersen and Chr. Sarauw issued their *Engelsk Begynderbog* ('English Primer'), which became very popular and was used well into the twentieth century.[24] There were other similar books, and Jespersen's campaign for reform was undoubtedly successful: in a short time, in spite of opposition, his books had largely crowded out the old type of textbook.

But Jespersen's activities were of course not confined to his endeavour to improve the teaching of English (and French) at the elementary and intermediate levels; as a university teacher from 1893 to 1925 he made an outstanding contribution towards raising the professional level of numerous future teachers of English. His achievement as a teacher has been aptly characterized as follows by one of his former students:

> As a teacher his influence was very great. He seldom lectured on literary subjects, but he had the admirable custom of giving lectures and taking classes on problems that were occupying his mind, giving his ideas a trial run before his students and inviting them to discuss them with him. This introduction into the workshop of a master was in itself almost a linguistic education. During a generation all the secondary school teachers of English received their training under his auspices and under his direct influence, and this

38

resulted in an enormous improvement of the standard of teaching in the schools.[25]

Otto Jespersen was a rationalist and a radical, and this basic attitude stamped all his work. One notes the same refreshing anti-dogmatism both in his views on language-teaching and in the way he approached English as an academic subject. He did pioneering work within phonetics, a comparatively new discipline which was then in rather low repute, and in his treatment of English syntax he largely discarded traditional concepts and terms in order 'to do justice to the real nature of grammatical phenomena'.[26] Occasionally his disrespect for traditional views led him astray; there are probably not many today who share his belief in 'progress in language'.[27] He was of course not the only one to be sceptical of tradition – he repeatedly acknowledged his debt to the kindred spirits referred to above. The inspiration and encouragement that he received from them fused with his own reforming zeal, enabling him to bring about improvements both in language-teaching and in the academic study of language.

Notes

1. See Inge Kabell & Hanne Lauridsen, 'Den første engelsk-danske ordbog (1678)', in *Publications on English Themes*, vol. 5, Department of English, University of Copenhagen 1987, pp. 57-72.

2. Peter Skautrup, *Det danske Sprogs Historie*, vol. III, Copenhagen 1953, p. 138; A. Henriques, *Shakespeare og Danmark indtil 1840*, Copenhagen 1941, p. 20. The first translator to tackle Shakespeare's English was Johannes Boye (1777); see Paul V. Rubow, *Shakespeare paa Dansk*, Copenhagen 1932, p. 10f.

3. *An English and Danish Dictionary...*, London 1754; here and elsewhere I have translated quotations from works written in Danish into English.

4. N.M. Petersen, 'Om sprogundervisning', in *Samlede Afhandlinger*, vol. 2, Copenhagen 1871, p. 220 (originally published in *Nordisk Ugeskrift* 1837).

5. *En sprogmands levned*, Copenhagen 1938, p. 46f.

6. There was, however, one area of English philology that had called forth a number of studies quite early in the nineteenth century, namely Old English; see on this Jørgen Erik Nielsen in *Københavns Universitet 1479-1979*, vol. IX, Copenhagen 1979, p. 271f.

7. Cf. O. Svanholt, *Bøger og metoder i dansk fremmedsprogundervisning. En historisk fremstilling*, Copenhagen 1968.

8. J. King (= Johann König), *The True English Guide...*, Copenhagen 1770. There are sporadic instances of this way of approaching English grammar even in the twentieth century; see Paul Christophersen's article in this volume, p. 7.

9. H.C.A. Lund, *Søkadet-Korpsets Historie 1701-1901*, Copenhagen 1901, p. 246.

10. Cf. Edmund Gosse's comment on the English of one of his Danish friends: 'the Dean talked English in a manner which betrayed a study of literature rather than daily intercourse with men. That is to say, he had a surprisingly wide vocabulary and a limited stock of idioms, so that the strangest combinations of fine antiquated language and rudimentary syntax amusingly presented themselves', in *Two Visits to Denmark, 1872, 1874,* London 1911, p. 26.

11. *En sprogmands levned*, p. 66.

12. A. Boysen, *Professor Listovs engelske system*, Copenhagen n.d., p. 99.

13. On Carl Mariboe see K.E. Bugge, *Skolen for livet. Studier over N. F.S. Grundtvigs pædagogiske tanker*, Copenhagen 1965, pp. 287-93, and *Dansk biografisk Leksikon*, third edition, vol. 9, Copenhagen 1981.

14. Svanholt, pp. 181ff., p. 248.

15. O. Jespersen, 'Den ny Sprogundervisnings Program', in *Vor Ungdom*, 1886, p. 363; *Sprogundervisning*, 1901, pp. 100ff. N.M. Petersen's views are to be found in his long article 'Sprogkundskab

i Norden', in *Samlede Afhandlinger*, vol. 2, p. 297f. (originally published in *Annaler for nordisk oldkyndighed* 1840-41).

16. *En sprogmands levned*, pp. 38ff.

17. *En sprogmands levned*, pp. 45ff.

18. See note 15 above.

19. The first edition appeared in 1901; an English version, *How to Teach a Foreign Language*, translated by Sophia Yhlen-Olsen Bertelsen, was first published in 1904; a revised, less polemical, second edition of *Sprogundervisning* appeared in 1935.

20. By way of illustration I give a few examples of this kind of transcription, taken from L. Meyer's *Fremmedordbog* (sixth edition, Copenhagen 1884) that may be considered to be typical; *baby* /bebi/, *church* /tsjørtsj/, *blunder* /blönder/, *shrub* /sjrob/, *counsel* /kovnsel/, *cloth* /klodh/, *dowager* /dovædsjer/, *measure* /messjur/.

21. E.F. Ancker, *Engelsk=Dansk Parleur*, Copenhagen 1856, p. 6.

22. *How to Teach a Foreign Language*, p. 111.

23. *How to Teach a Foreign Language*, p. 57.

24. See Paul Christophersen's comments on it in this volume, p. 1.

25. C.A. Bodelsen, *Essays and Papers*, Copenhagen 1964, p. 188f.

26. O. Jespersen, *A Modern English Grammar on Historical Principles*, vol. IV, Preface, Copenhagen 1931.

27. First voiced in his thesis of 1891 and repeated in his last published book, *Efficiency in Linguistic Change*, Copenhagen 1941. See Hans Frede Nielsen's article in this volume.

Jørgen Rischel

OTTO JESPERSEN'S CONTRIBUTION
TO DANISH AND GENERAL PHONETICS

Otto Jespersen's outstanding international reputation in linguistics seems first and foremost to be associated with his work on the history of English and his contributions to theoretical syntax, although it is also generally recognized that he did pioneering research on child language and on several topics which can be subsumed under the label 'applied linguistics'.

This variegated picture of Jespersen as a philologist and linguist is further complicated by the fact that in his early career he also established himself as a leading representative of classical phonetics. In this capacity he made a strong and lasting impact on the approach adopted by linguists and dialectologists in Denmark and more widely in Scandinavia, in particular with regard to the use of practical phonetic transcription as a tool in descriptive and didactic work.

Nineteenth-century phonetics had a fourfold origin, which it may be useful to outline here before proceeding to an account of Jespersen's contribution.

Firstly, it had developed out of the philosophical grammar inherited from Antiquity, which contained a section on 'letters'. Philosophical grammar was at first concerned with the classical languages, but the scope was eventually widened, although in some quarters it took a very long time to realize that contemporary spoken languages are just as structured as the written classical languages. Over the centuries valuable contributions were made to the phonetic description of modern languages such as English and Danish.

Secondly, along with this philosophical interest in speech sounds there developed a concern with the physics and physiology of speech, which occasionally led to technological applications as in the attempts

43

in the eighteenth century to construct talking machines. In the second half of the nineteenth century physicists and physiologists applied rigid methods from the natural sciences to the study of speech sounds, and such studies were also taken up by a few enthusiastic linguists, although the technology was altogether very limited (and remained so up to the Second World War).

Thirdly, with the development of comparative and historical linguistics in the early nineteenth century there came an upsurge of interest in phonetics as it had developed out of philosophical grammar. In order to understand sound shifts it was necessary to have an adequate taxonomy of speech sounds and an adequate phonetic alphabet. Rasmus Rask, for one, devoted much of his short lifetime to phonetic issues. About the time when the neogrammarian trend came into prominence the physical and physiological approach to phonetics (see above) came to play an important role in furnishing an allegedly scientific basis for linguistics.

Finally, the national romantic movement in the early and mid-nineteenth century, which gave an impetus to the development of historical linguistics, also triggered a concern for contemporary local languages or dialects. These were studied intensively for the purpose of showing that they were genuine continuations of ancient idioms, but also with a more practical aim: that of raising them to the status of real languages by devising a practical orthography. In Scandinavia this manifested itself partly in studies of neglected languages such as Faroese and Finnish and Lappish, and partly in studies of the dialects contained within status languages such as Danish. Norwegian dialectology was established in the nineteenth century in more or less close association with the endeavours to establish 'landsmål' as a written language. As a separate linguistic discipline *dialectology* developed its own need for accurate phonetic transcription.

Needless to say, the four roots of modern phonetics outlined here were not rigidly separated: it is more a matter of differences in goals and scientific approaches than of rigidly separated scientific milieus. What is characteristic of the late nineteenth century was *the convergence of these various trends* into phonetics in a wider sense. Unfortunately this convergence tended to result in exaggerated emphasis on 'scientific' accuracy in the handling of speech sounds at the expense of structural analysis.

Phonetics in the late nineteenth century was first and foremost developed by British scholars. In France and Germany there had been a pronounced interest in the physiology of speech and singing for a long time, but phonetics in a narrower sense was only about to become a scientific discipline. In Germany the study of speech physiology developed into real descriptive phonetics with the work of E. Sievers (*Grundzüge der Lautphysiologie*, 1876), who was later strongly influenced by the British school of phoneticians. In France Paul Passy played a role both as a teacher of phonetics and as editor of the periodical *Le maître phonétique* (the journal of the 'association phonétique des professeurs des langues vivantes'). In France, too, experimental phonetics (or rather, as Jespersen says, 'machine phonetics') developed rapidly around the turn of the century with Abbé Rousselot as the prominent figure, though at the beginning it met with a fair amount of scepticism elsewhere. Still, England held the dominant position. Phoneticians such as Ellis, Bell and Sweet (and later Daniel Jones) were from the start oriented towards the concrete task of specifying speech sounds, and the design of a practical phonetic transcription system. It is well known that the collaboration of English and French scholars (Henry Sweet, Paul Passy) resulted in the introduction and spread of the phonetic alphabet of the International Phonetic Association (IPA). Sweet in particular was also influential in Scandinavia. Two admirers of his, the Norwegian Johan Storm and his younger Danish colleague Otto Jespersen (who was much influenced by Storm), although experts on the English language, were active in research on their mother tongues as well. They each designed a national phonetic alphabet, viz. the 'Norvegia' and the 'Dania' systems of transcription. Their orientation towards Sweet's conception of phonetics contributed substantially to the high degree of activity and the high level of scholarship attained by descriptive phonetics and dialectology in these countries.

Denmark, like England, has a very long record of phonetic research (cf. Eli Fischer-Jørgensen: 'Fonetik', in *Københavns Universitet 1479-1979* vol. IX, 1979). Empirical work started with the sixteenth-century theologian Jacob Madsen Aarhus, who wrote a learned book *De Litteris* in which he made interesting observations on contemporary Danish (Jutlandish) pronunciation. Later, in the eighteenth century, another Dane,Jens P. Høysgaard, who held a junior post at the University of Copenhagen, wrote authoritative monographs on Danish grammar, including a very important analysis of Danish prosody. In the nineteenth century Rasmus Rask, who concerned himself with universal aspects of speech sounds and with the development of phonetically based orthographies, also did empirical work on his own dialect. His near-contemporary Jacob Hornemann Bredsdorff wrote a seminal paper on the causes of sound change. Later, towards the turn of the century, physiological and even acoustic phonetics began to develop as a component of linguistic scholarship and attracted the attention of Danish linguists such as Vilhelm Thomsen and Karl Verner. Verner was particularly interested in experimental methods and corresponded on this topic with the linguist and acoustician Hugo Pipping in Finland; he also wrote a paper on the Danish *stød*. Julius Hoffory gave lectures on 'language physiology' at the University of Copenhagen, but they were discontinued after he got a chair in phonetics in Berlin in the eighties. Meanwhile dialectology in Denmark had reached a high level of scholarship with K. J. Lyngby, who in the fifties had designed a very good transcription system for Danish dialects. Both then and later there was close and fruitful contact between Danish dialectologists and the leading scholars in comparative and theoretical linguistics; Thomsen, for example, wrote the phonetic introduction to J. C. S. Espersen's dictionary of the dialect of Bornholm (published posthumously in 1908).

Otto Jespersen's achievements in phonetics must be seen on this basis. He derived his interest in phonetics from Henry Sweet's *Handbook of Phonetics* (1877), and as early as in 1881 he attended lectures on phonetics given by Vilhelm Thomsen. Even when Jespersen was still a student, Thomsen encouraged him to publish various reviews of textbooks on phonetics, and the two remained in contact over this subject during Jespersen's travels to England, Germany and France in the late eighties. During his stay in Paris Jespersen became close friends with the distinguished young French phonetician Paul Passy. Jespersen soon had an expert knowledge of the accumulated phonetic scholarship in these countries, and in 1897-9 he published his extensive compendium of descriptive phonetics: *Fonetik, En systematisk fremstilling af læren om sproglyd* (636 pages). It appeared first in Danish, but was soon afterwards revised and published in German as well (*Phonetische Grundfragen*, 1904, which covers some of the topics; and *Lehrbuch der Phonetik*, 1904, with subsequent editions up to 1932).

This work is an excellent presentation of what we now refer to as 'classical phonetics'. At the same time it is interesting that Jespersen – as he already emphasizes in the Preface – bases the exposition on his own first-hand observations and his own thinking on the subject. As he states explicitly, he knows Danish best, then English; in the third place come French and German, and in the fourth Norwegian, Swedish, Faroese, Icelandic, Italian and some other languages. He claims that he rarely speaks about sounds which he has not been able to imitate to the satisfaction of native speakers, and never about sounds that he has not heard several times. Even so, the reader is warned in the Preface not to trust any single piece of information about a sound in a language (including Danish) without checking and rechecking with native informants.

The book *Fonetik* is also a landmark in Danish phonetics because of its terminology. Jespersen has contributed more than anyone else to Danish phonetic terminology. Some of his innovations had appeared in his earlier writings but many occur for the first time in *Fonetik*. For the most part they are part and parcel of the education of students of phonetics in Denmark to this day. His new terminology seems to have had two separate motivations.

Firstly, Jespersen advocated a terminology which as far as possible was Danish, such as *hæmme* (constriction). This continued a trend which has a strong hold among Danish linguists (it started long before Jespersen with Høysgaard and Rask), though today we are possibly not

Jørgen Rischel

altogether happy with the coexistence of synonymous international and Danish terms in scientific work. Secondly, however, he introduced new articulatory terms which attempted to clarify the notions and avoid misleading metaphors. In this attempt he has been partially successful: for example, no Danish student of language today would refer to a sound as 'guttural', but philologists still speak about 'cerebral' sounds (both of these terms are criticized by Jespersen on p. 206). He mentions that *betoning* when referring to accentuation is a particularly harmful term (Jespersen uses *tryk*, i.e. stress), but we must admit that even today *betoning* is frequently used (ironically, it has been found that 'stress' in Danish, as in many other languages, is not so much a matter of intensity but has an important tonal component).

In principle Jespersen was quite right in his criticism of the then current phonetic terminology in western countries. Although the understanding of articulatory phonetics had advanced considerably a hundred years ago, the terminology was (and in many quarters still is) a strange mixture of precise articulatory terms side by side with pseudoarticulatory terms such as 'guttural' mentioned above, with kinaesthetic or metaphorical expressions such as 'liquid', and with impressionistic auditory terms such as 'sibilant'. Jespersen contributed substantially to the establishment of a consistent terminology based on the configurations of the vocal tract during the articulation of each speech sound.

As a framework for the specification of articulatory states Jespersen as early as in the eighties developed a kind of visible speech which he called the 'analphabetic system' (*The Articulations of Speech Sounds Represented by Means of Analphabetic Symbols*, 1889; later, to avoid ridicule, it was christened the 'antalphabetic system'). In this he was obviously inspired by similar endeavours on the part of British phoneticians, notably Melville Bell (father of Graham Bell, the inventor of the telephone). Briefly stated, the idea is to indicate separately the part of the speech organs that moves, the part it moves in relation to, and the type of passage between them. To accomplish this he uses: (i) ordinary letters to indicate the passive articulator at a constriction (e.g. 'e' for the inner side of the upper front teeth, and 'f' for the alveolar ridge involved e.g. in ar-

48

ticulating [t], [l] or [s]), (ii) Greek letters for the active articulator at the constriction (e.g. 'ß' for the tip of the tongue articulating in such sounds), and (iii) numerals and other characters for the degree and shape of the aperture at a place of constriction (e.g. 'ß0' for closure as in [t], 'ß1' for a groove in the tongue as in [s], 'ßI' for a lateral passage as in [l]). This system opens the possibility for one and the same anatomical feature to be labelled differently in different cases; for example, the uvula is a passive articulator in uvular consonants but an active articulator in nasalized sounds. The dynamics of articulation and of the airstream are indicated by additional symbols.

Today probably nobody uses this system, and few people refer to it, although similar notions play a role in discussions of the quantal nature of articulation and of modern distinctive feature theory. What remains of direct practical value is his wealth of precise articulatory description of sound types. These descriptions were based on extremely simple methods of direct observation, partly with the help of the ear. On the whole Jespersen was not particularly interested in instrumental phonetics.

This appears even more clearly in his attitude towards those who studied the physics (acoustics) of speech sounds. In his *Fonetik* he devotes several pages to a discussion of the pros and cons of articulatory versus physical approaches to phonetic description. His point of departure is the claim, widely made at the time, that with regard to speech sounds articulation is the cause and acoustics the effect. As a consequence the former should be considered primary in relation to the latter; this contention was supported with reference to sound change (e.g. assimilation), which was considered to be rooted in sound production rather than acoustics. On the opposite side scholars like Pipping claimed the primacy of the acoustic properties of speech sounds for phonetic specification (note that in more recent time Roman Jakobson has made the contention that 'we speak in order to be heard in order to be understood', which would seem to give the primacy to sound perception). Jespersen very judiciously attaches proper importance to all phases of the oral communication act: 'H1' (*hjerne* no.1, i.e. the speaker's brain), 'M' (*mund*, i.e. his speech organs), 'L' (*luft*, i.e. the air, and other transmission media), 'Ø' (*øre*, i.e. the auditory apparatus), and 'H2' (*hjerne* no.2, i.e. the listener's brain). He rightly points out that a linguistic change must be transmitted many times via the path 'M-L-Ø' in order to gain ground, and that language acquisition by children cannot take place in any other way than via this transmission path.

A scientific system must build on *constant* features of the phenomena under study, says Jespersen. The question, then, is whether such constancy is more likely to be found in articulatory or in acoustic phonetics. Jespersen finds that the search for constancy poses problems in both areas (this, incidentally, is a live issue in modern phonetics). Still, he finds reasons to be most sceptical concerning the results of acoustic phonetic analyses, which often seem contradictory, and hence he prefers to put the main emphasis on articulatory specifications. Jespersen also makes the point that acoustic analysis has a serious limitation by dealing only with what happens in the air; we do not know enough about what happens in the ear, and how the auditory impression is processed by the brain. The latter, says Jespersen, is in fact intimately connected with articulation (and thus in his view rather supports the articulatory approach to phonetics: the recognition of speech sounds is the very basis for investigation of their articulation). In the context of this lengthy discussion Jespersen makes several pertinent observations, particularly with regard to the alleged close connection between articulation and sound impression (which is a central issue in the so-called Motor Theory of Speech Perception proposed by the American Haskins group of researchers after the Second World War). Jespersen also speculates about the importance of this articulation-perception linkage for language acquisition (he assumes that through babbling the child quite early learns certain fixed associations between articulations and auditory impressions). In spite of these observations it is fair to say that Jespersen grossly underrated the importance of acoustics for the study of phonetic phenomena. The section on speech acoustics is in fact the only part of his compendium which is entirely obsolete today (Eli Fischer-Jørgensen, *loc. cit.* p. 410).

Otto Jespersen's Contribution to Phonetics

Danish phonetics owes a great debt to Otto Jespersen. As already mentioned, there is a wealth of information on Danish in his *Fonetik*, and he later wrote papers on various topics such as the *stød*. Most influential was his booklet *Modersmålets fonetik* ('Phonetics of the mother tongue') which appeared in numerous editions from 1906 onwards and was still used as the standard textbook when this writer took a course in Danish phonetics at the University of Copenhagen. In addition to lucidly written sections on the speech sounds of Danish it has even more interesting sections on Danish prosody. Jespersen has important novel observations on virtually all aspects of Danish phonetics but it is especially interesting to see what he has to say about *stress* and the extent to which he manages to identify and label the syntactico-semantico-pragmatic ('logical', 'psychological') conditions for specific types of stress patterns. In the decades after Jespersen's pioneering research little was done about this topic, which seemed rather peripheral in the context of a structural analysis of the language; it is only at the present time that Danish linguists and phoneticians are really struggling to arrive at a deeper understanding of prosody as part of the 'interface' between expression and meaning.

It is time now to have a brief look at Jespersen's role in descriptive dialectology in Denmark.

Jespersen's influence is essentially connected with his phonetic notation system, the 'Dania' as it is called because it was first published in the journal *Dania* (vol. I, 1890-). Almost all practical work in Danish dialectology up to this day has been based on the use of this notation. In addition, Jespersen was more directly influential by the assistance he gave to his contemporaries and of course also as a teacher of English phonetics (at first also of Danish phonetics) at the University of Copenhagen.

Jespersen's ideas aroused the interest of Danish scholars even in his very young days. When in 1886 the nestor of early Danish folklore studies and dialectology, the Reverend H. F. Feilberg, began to publish his monumental Jutlandish dialect dictionary (*Bidrag til en ordbog over jyske almuesmål*), this happened a little too early for Jespersen's new notation system for Danish to be adopted. Feilberg had to use the traditional Lyngby system but was clearly aware that it would soon be outdated. He refers to Lyngby's notation as 'undoubtedly trailblazing for its time', but then goes on to mention that Jespersen had done him the favour of working out a comparison between that system and the new system proposed by Jespersen himself, the 'Dania' system (his character-by-character comparison is printed in Feilberg's introduction pp. X-XI; for a comparison of the Dania with other Nordic dialect alphabets and with the IPA see *Nordisk Lærebog for Talepædagoger* 1954, p. 306a-d). I think this is characteristic of Jespersen's prestige even at this early stage of his career. – When Feilberg was presented with a Festschrift on his eightieth anniversary in 1911, Jespersen saluted him with an essay on the grammar of cursing and swearing.

Among the dialectologists who in early works acknowledged more direct assistance from Jespersen in their work are Nikolaj Andersen, who wrote a treatise on the tonal accent in the East Slesvig dialect (*Dania,* vol. IV, 1897), and J. M. Jensen, whose monograph on the North Jutland dialect (*Et Vendelbomåls Lyd- og Formlære,* 1897–1902) is one of the first to use Jespersen's new system for the purpose of narrow phonetic transcription. The dialect survey *Kort over danske Folkemål,* which appeared from 1898 onwards, uses the Dania transcription, which was thus becoming the reference notation for Danish dialectologists by the turn of the century.

Scholars working on the other languages spoken within the national boundaries of Denmark were also directly influenced by Jespersen. A particularly early example is the phonetic notation for Faroese in V.U. Hammershaimb's *Færøsk Anthologi* (1891). The sections on dialects and vocabulary were written by the young Faroese Jakob Jakobsen (who later acquired fame for his work on Orkney and Shetland Norn). Jakobsen's linguistic approach, for which he acknowledges the assistance that he had got from Otto Jespersen and from Vilhelm Thomsen, is impressive. The Faroese anthology is a book for both the lay and the learned, but the contributions by Jakobsen certainly have a different flavour from the rest. His precise phonetic definitions of the speech sounds of Faroese (based to a large extent on Sweet's English terminology) are outstanding as is the resulting phonetic notation.

William Thalbitzer was a somewhat later pupil of Jespersen's. He was a Nordic philologist but went to Greenland in 1901 in order to make a phonetic study of West Greenlandic Eskimo. He soon became the leading authority on Eskimo of his time. Since Thalbitzer put so much emphasis on phonetics, and since possibly he was one of the best-known scholars who learned practical phonetics from Otto Jespersen, it is necessary to mention here that in fact he did not live up to Jespersen's standards at all. Thalbitzer had learned about phonetic notation and about direct observation of articulation (he proudly describes how he put things into the informants' mouths to feel the position of the tongue). However, although he made many fine observations he seems to have lacked Jespersen's and other eminent linguists' intuition about *relevance and consistency* as prerequisites to linguistic documentation by means of phonetic notation. His transcriptions – especially in the very earliest work, *A Phonetical Study of the Eskimo Language Based on Observations Made on a Journey in North Greenland* (1904) – are often a messy mixture of systematic features and accidental variations. – When this Jespersenian phonetic notation was later taken over by the explorer and anthropologist Knud Rasmussen, the result was actually in some cases rather more felicitous, since Rasmussen, being a native speaker of Greenlandic, had the intuition about phonological structure which is so important for a consistent use of phonetic notation.

In spite of his vast experience in listening and taking down word forms in phonetic notation, Jespersen was not himself much of a field worker. He was immensely influential in dialectology, but unlike many other Danish philologists of his time he seems to have participated very little in the first-hand recording of Danish dialects. There is, however, an interesting corpus of data on Danish pronunciation which Jørn Lund has analysed ('Studier i dansk sceneudtale, Otto Jespersens bidrag til teatersproghistorien', *Festskrift til Kristian Hald* 1974, pp. 461-72). This is a set of notebooks in which Jespersen took down pronunciation forms during theatre performances in Copenhagen in 1895-7, that is, just about the time when he wrote his *Fonetik*. There are of course notes about forms which deviated more or less from everyday pronunciation, but there are also notes which serve to illustrate well-known phonetic processes in Danish such as assimilation and cluster simplification (these notes obviously had an immediate purpose as raw material for his phonetics textbooks).

There is a more interesting angle to this corpus of notes about actors' speech, however. Lund aptly points out that Jespersen's notes are not specifically concerned with formal style (which, of course, one might expect actors to use) and that he did not even concentrate on special pronunciations *per se* but seems to have taken great interest in the *range of variation* in the use of Danish that he could hear from the stage. Linguistic variation was a topic of much theoretical importance to Jespersen (as it is to contemporary linguists after decades of principled neglect in structural linguistics) but it was also a central issue in his attacks on popular beliefs about 'correct' or 'vulgar' speech. One of the topics under focus is the use of truncated forms of function words (auxiliaries, prepositions, and the like): *ka* for *kan*, and so on. In his notebooks Jespersen has an endless stream of notes about such forms, and as Lund points out, this should be understood in connection with his statement in *Fonetik* (pp. 119-20) about the frequent use of such forms even by all the leading actors. Nowhere, says Jespersen, do people find it more difficult to observe than in this very area. It was essential for him to have empirical verification for his attack on prejudices about the 'vulgarity' of such pronunciations. – As for the question of a prescribed norm he concludes (in his *Fonetik*, p. 90) that one cannot easily use the pronunciation of actors as the norm, since one may encounter different pronunciations of the same word on the stage. Rather, he says, actors should learn in real life what is the best pronunciation, and they should use that pronunciation on the stage (except when special circumstances call for deviations from it).

One of the most tangible applications of Jespersen's phonetic competence was in the field of foreign language didactics. He wrote a textbook of English phonetics for Danish university students, but language teaching in grammar schools was one of the areas of debate in which he played the most prominent role with his emphasis on proficiency in the speaking of modern languages. Language teaching as such is outside the topic of the present paper, but it deserves mention here that he insisted on the use of phonetic notation as the first type of written language which the child encounters when learning English. His own English primer (which is no longer used) is based on this principle and thus made generations of Danish school children familiar with phonetic symbols at an early age. Incidentally, Jespersen wrote a comment on Craigie's system for the acquisition of English pronunciation and orthography by foreigners (W. A. Craigie: *English Reading Made Easy*, 1922; *An Advanced English Reader*, 1924). Craigie considered it better to use an orthography provided with extra diacritic symbols to indicate pronunciation rather than to have two totally separate representations, one phonetic and the other conventionally orthographic. He had followers in various countries. Jespersen (whose comment appeared in *Vor Ungdom* ['Our Youth'], 1926) argues that his own phonetic notation requires the learning of only a few symbols (nine letters and two diacritics) which do not occur in the standard orthography, whereas Craigie's system used some fifty additional symbols. More importantly, however, he takes issue with one of the arguments against the full use of phonetic notation, viz. that the use of phonetic notation is a roundabout way of learning the standard orthography. It is a mistake to think that only written English is 'real English', says Jespersen: in fact it is not the written form but rather the spoken language that is primary. Both must be learned, but unlike the written symbol the speech sound disappears the moment it is produced. Phonetic notation is a means of recording it so that it can be learned and remembered.

In his later years Jespersen did not concern himself much with phonetics in his research and in his writings, although he updated his textbook of Danish phonetics in important ways, e.g. by going into more detail over the phonetics of Danish dialects (in the 2nd edition) and by including a 'phonological survey' of Danish speech sounds and their combinatorial possibilities (in the 3rd edition, 1936). – He played a role in the International Phonetic Association, and in the mid-twenties he was involved in revising the IPA alphabet (recommendations of the 'Copenhagen Conference' of phoneticians), but the proposed changes were on the whole not widely accepted (a revision is still called for, and a new conference will finally take place in 1989).

Jespersen never came round to publishing his *magnum opus* on general phonetics in English. However, at one point it was planned that Hans Jørgen Uldall, the brilliant practical phonetician and language theoretician, who was quite young at that time, should revise the *Lehrbuch* with English-speaking readers in mind (later the planned work was referred to as 'Essentials of Phonetics', which translates the title of Jespersen's other early book, *Phonetische Grundfragen*). In October 1928 Jespersen wrote to Uldall to tell him that Daniel Jones was somewhat troubled over the plan because it might delay Uldall's studies at University College London. In 1935 they discussed various points (modifications of the an(t)alphabetic system, degrees of stress, and other topics).

In the late thirties Jespersen (with reference to his own advanced age) expressed some jealousy over Uldall's collaboration with Louis Hjelmslev: 'Hjelmslev is young and he can wait better than I can'. In 1938 or 1939 the plan was changed; now it was to be a joint venture: *'Essentials of Phonetics and Phonology* [altered from: *with remarks on phonology*] by Otto Jespersen and Hans Jørgen Uldall'. We know that although Jespersen was in a sense a forerunner of phonology with his emphasis on the distinctive function of speech sounds (Eli Fischer-Jørgensen, *loc.cit.* p. 410), he was not much impressed by the phonologists' 'complicated terminology', nor by Hjelmslev's deductive theory of glossematics ('I do not yet really understand what it means to approach phonetics deductively, any more than a zoologist can describe carnivorous animals deductively' (my translation)). It thus looks as if the lay-out was really a concession to Uldall. Anyway, the war broke out and the work was never completed.

In order now to take stock of the ways in which Otto Jespersen has influenced modern phonetics in a wider sense, it may be useful to list a number of distinct though more or less overlapping areas within phonetics proper or within applied phonetics. The following is of course not to be understood as an exhaustive listing:

   (i)   Systems (taxonomies) for descriptive labelling of speech sounds; phonetic alphabets;

   (ii)   Documentary phonetic transcription of linguistic specimens;

   (iii)   Phonetics and language policy – normative pronouncing dictionaries;

   (iv)   Application of phonetics to foreign language teaching;

   (v)   Study of the phonetic aspect of language acquisition;

   (vi)   Phonetics as a component of historical/comparative language studies;

   (vii)   General theories about sound change and the causes of sound change;

   (viii)   Study of the expressive/aesthetic function of speech sounds;

   (ix)   Analysis of sound patterns with regard to linguistic function (phonology); the expression system of language as a social convention or as a cognitive pattern;

   (x)   Typology and universals of sounds and sound patterns;

   (xi)   Study of speech production: observable behaviour of the speech organs and underlying neural control;

   (xii)   The acoustics of speech;

   (xiii)   Study of the perception of speech: phenomenological (psychological) and neurophysiological aspects;

   (xiv)   General methodological and metatheoretical aspects of phonetics and phonology.

If we look at this list, it is clear that with the exception of item (i) – which is a prerequisite of practical phonetic work – it is the last several items, viz. (vii)–(xiv), that constitute the core of general phonetics/phonology proper. Otto Jespersen touched on all of these core issues in his writings, and he used phonetics extensively in his historical studies of English (cf. item (vi)). However, I think it is fair to say that his main contribution within the phonetic sciences was to 'practical phonetics' (items (i)–(ii)) and to 'applied phonetics' in a wide sense (cf. items (iii) –(vi)), although he had a much broader view of language than, for example, his younger English colleague Daniel Jones (in his autobiography *En sprogmands levned*, 1938, p. 219, Jespersen mentions the excessively practical and non-theoretical bias of Jones's approach as stated in the latter's brief paper 'The Aims of Phonetics' of 1937). It is Jespersen's amazing breadth in these studies, paired with his never failing linguistic intuition as a safeguard against errors or downright nonsense, which impresses the reader today.

On the whole, reflections on metatheoretical issues do not loom large in Jespersen's strictly phonetic writings, which mostly belong to his earliest career, though they bear the stamp of the judicious scholar who was familiar with all aspects of language. As a descriptive phonetician he was a practical positivist and down-to-earth humanistic scholar who placed direct observation and common-sense descriptive methods higher than sophisticated instrumental methods purporting to disclose the nature of speech sounds, and higher than the phonologists' speculations about sound patterns (Brøndal's work in this area did not appeal to him, for example). However, if we make a comparison with the contemporaneous use of the Swedish dialect alphabet with its non-systematic handling of excessive phonetic detail and phonetic variation, Jespersen can be seen to have been firmly rooted in the linguistically more sober tradition of Danish dialectology. In his pioneering work in this very area he avoided the worst pitfalls of pre-phonological practical phonetics by largely sticking to languages he knew well and was able to speak himself. Not all of the colleagues who learned from him were equally fortunate in their phonetic transcription, as we have seen above with regard to Thalbitzer in particular.

It is not surprising that the advent of the Hjelmslev school with its emphasis on formal patterns in language analysis meant a cleavage in Danish phonetics and dialectology. Eventually, Danish dialectology adopted several components of the Hjelmslevian paradigm (entailing an emphasis on abstract form which has hardly been productive in the long run). In general phonetics the work of Eli Fischer-Jørgensen over a broad spectrum of phonetic issues has meant a great boom in the application of instrumental methods to phonetic research, and at the same time she has made seminal contributions to the integration of linguistics and phonetics. Thus, except for the continued use of the Dania system of phonetic transcription in dialect studies, Otto Jespersen does not play a very direct role in present-day phonetics and dialectology in Denmark.

In another sense, however, Otto Jespersen still has direct followers today, as witness the monumental two-volume monograph on the development of spoken Standard Danish since 1840, *Dansk Rigsmål* (1975), written by Lars Brink and Jørn Lund. It provoked considerable debate among Danish phoneticians, partly because of the different ideas that are held about research paradigms but also because its impressionistic analyses in some cases run counter to the assumptions (or prejudices) about Danish pronunciation that were shared by most of us. By its impressive wealth of detailed observations, this work is indeed a continuation of Jespersen's phonetic scholarship.

At the same time it is conspicuous how little Brink and Lund have done about confronting their empirical approach and their basic contentions with contemporary linguistic and sociolinguistic theory. Still, it is refreshing that such a piece of work should have appeared and illuminated essential aspects of Danish pronunciation in an almost revolutionary way. This is certainly more in the spirit of Otto Jespersen's scholarship than was the degenerate use of phonetic transcription in the study of Danish which the present author experienced as a young student at the University of Copenhagen. At that time one of the formal requirements in the undergraduate course in Danish language was that the student must be able to convert a text in standard orthography into normative phonetic transcription. That obviously involved two skills: (i) mastering the conventions of an orthoepic algorithm that transformed spelling into a very conservative pronunciation, and (ii) internalization of the specific pronunciation of individual Danish words in this conservative standard pronunciation.

Such training helped students from different social and geographical backgrounds to become thoroughly familiar with a prescribed norm, but it did not of course teach them how to observe what Danes really say when they speak (apparently this was supposed to be of interest mainly to speech therapists, except when it was a question of real dialect). Much later, when teaching such a course at another Danish university, this writer was reluctantly permitted to base the test on the transcription of tape recordings instead, but it was emphasized that the recording should of course represent an acceptable style of Standard Danish. Not much, alas, was left of Jespersen's radicalism and of his empiricism in the approach to the phonetic study of the mother tongue!

Today we experience the integration of a multitude of empirical approaches, of observational studies and formal analyses, and of basic and applied research, e.g. in variational studies. Against this perspective Jespersen's broad-mindedness and his pioneering spirit in phonetics more than half a century ago should not be forgotten. In more than one sense he made lasting contributions to the phonetic sciences.

Acknowledgement: I wish to thank Marie Bjerrum, Frans Gregersen, Bent Jul Nielsen and Elizabeth Uldall for valuable information on Jespersen's scholarly contacts.

Hans Frede Nielsen

ON OTTO JESPERSEN'S VIEW OF LANGUAGE EVOLUTION

I

The importance of Otto Jespersen as a language historian is reflected in a number of ways. His *Growth and Structure of the English Language* (*GSEL*), which first appeared in 1905 and which came in as many as nine editions within a span of 33 years, is probably the most widely read introduction to the history of the English language ever written. Later impressions of the ninth edition have ensured that the book, although dated in some respects, is being used even today. The popularity of *GSEL* should be at least partly ascribed to Jespersen's qualities as scholar and teacher: he vividly illustrates the dependence of language development on cultural and political history and explains language changes in a clear and, on the whole, undogmatic and intelligent way, often sprinkling his account with specimens of a very personal sense of humour.

The scholarly height of Jespersen's career – and not only in terms of language history – was the publication of *A Modern English Grammar on Historical Principles* (*MEG*) 1909-49, which along with the works of Visser (1963-73) and Mustanoja (1960) is thought by Rydén (1979:25) to belong to the 'most important contributions' to (traditional) English historical syntax. As a matter of fact, Rydén thinks that *MEG* exhibits 'the most original analyses' of all, even if he deplores Jespersen's occasional mixing of synchronic and diachronic considerations and the 'paucity' of texts examined for some periods (1979:26). Rydén is probably right (also) in the latter point of his criticism, which need not be at variance with the immediate experience of most users of *MEG*: that the work is a quarry of detailed information and carefully selected examples from the 15th century to the present age.

There have been countless references to *MEG*, *GSEL* and other of Jespersen's publications by scholars working in the same field. Well-known recent histories of the English language such as Strang (1970), Baugh & Cable (1978) and Pyles & Algeo (1982) all refer to him repeatedly as do the proceedings of international conferences on English historical linguistics published within the last few years, cf. Blake & Jones (1984) and Eaton et al. (1985). In his *Linguistic Evolution with Special Reference to English*, Samuels (1972:3) like Jespersen dissociates himself from what the latter called the 'all-or-nothing fallacy', i.e. the failure to acknowledge that a linguistic change can be the result of multiple conditioning, a concept that is well known to e.g. natural scientists. Samuels refers to Jespersen's *Language* (1922:262), but might have referred to much earlier works for practical examples of the operation of the principle of multiple conditioning. I am thinking especially of the 21 factors listed by Jespersen in his doctoral dissertation (*Studier over engelske kasus* (*SEK*) 1891:108-65, cf. *Progress in Language* (*PL*) 1894:186-272) for explaining case-shiftings in the pronouns. See also *GSEL* ((1905:179) 1938a:169). Another important discovery of Jespersen's, which was also first presented in *SEK* (1891:170-217), cf. also *Linguistica* 1933b:346-83 and *MEG* I, 1909:199-208, and which has often been dealt with in the scholarly literature, is 'Jespersen's Law'. By this is meant the change in the 15th and 16th centuries of *f, s, þ, ks, tʃ* to *v, z, ð, gz, dʒ* under conditions similar to those governing Verner's Law (after a weakly stressed vowel/syllable), an explanation accepted by prominent scholars like Luick (1921-40:§763 and §798), Schibsbye (1972:§9.01) and others.

Before embarking on a presentation of Jespersen's general concept of language evolution, I would like to round off these introductory remarks by drawing attention to Jespersen's insistence from the very first on observation as the basis of his scholarship. His treatment of e.g. the English group genitive in *PL* (1894:279-327) is a paragon of a well-organized, empirically-based historical account with well-chosen illustrative examples, foreshadowing in its method the volumes of *MEG* (in fact, Jespersen's treatment of the group genitive in *MEG* VI (1942:vi, ch. 17) is based on that in *PL*). Jespersen's insistence on an inductive approach has some bearing on his view of linguistic evolution in that he refused to accept theories which were not compatible with observable phenomena in especially present-day language (cf. 1891:36). He preferred to stay 'i virkelighedens fulde dagslys for der at studere livets gyldne træ' (1891:66), to move 'wholly in the broad daylight of history' (*Efficiency in Linguistic Change (ELC)* 1941:85).

II

Jespersen's views on linguistic evolution should be seen as a reaction against especially Schleicher's theory of language development. According to Schleicher, the historical development of any language is a story of decay, by which he means linguistic (phonetic) reduction. Chinese, which signifies neither stem-function nor flexional forms, is a particularly striking case, and modern languages like French and German show much attrition in comparison with Latin and Gothic respectively:

> ... unsere Worte nehmen sich gotischen gegenüber aus, wie etwas eine Statue, die durch langes Rollen in einem Flussbette um ihre Glieder gekommen und von der nicht viel mehr als eine abgeschliffene Steinwalze mit schwachen Andeutungen des einst vorhandenen geblieben ist; ein gotisches *habaidêdeima* lautet jetzt *hätten*, english gar nur *had* ...
>
> (Schleicher 1869:34)

Conversely, the further back in the history of a language we move, the higher the degree of linguistic perfection. Nevertheless Schleicher presupposes a development towards higher linguistic forms subsequent to the genesis of a language, but these higher forms were established during the pre-historical era of the language. Schleicher thinks that only peoples or tribes with fully developed languages could make their entrance into history, at which point language – being no longer an aim in itself – had become a vehicle of expressing intellectual activity. Schleicher further believes that an abundance of historical events will accelerate language decay, which explains why English among all the Germanic languages, '... in Laut und Form die stärksten Einbussen erlitten hat ...' (1869:35).

On all points, Jespersen takes the opposite view of Schleicher. As we saw above, theories which have no possibility of empirical substantiation are certainly not to his liking. And the claim that modern languages like English and French are less perfect than Gothic and Latin is attributed to Schleicher's admiration for the classical languages and a corresponding contempt for the modern vernacular languages.

With reference to Wilhelm von Humboldt's emphasis on languages as a means of communication, Jespersen (1891:9) instead suggests that the language which reaches the highest degree of communicative effectiveness with the fewest or simplest means is superior to other languages (cf. also 1894:13 and 1922:324). Thus Modern English *had* is infinitely preferable to Gothic *habaidêdeima* as anybody would agree who had to walk one mile instead of four (1891:11): *had* corresponds to 15 different Gothic forms (representing three persons, three numbers and two moods), and in terms of simplicity and economy this makes English vastly superior to Gothic. Jespersen therefore does not accept Schleicher's description of *had* and German *hätten* as worn-out relics of a perfect statue:

> What if, on the one hand [the statue] was not ornamental enough as a work of art, and if, on the other hand, human well-being was at stake if it was not serviceable in a rolling-mill: which would then be the better, – a rugged and unwieldy statue, making difficulties at every rotation, or an even, smooth, easy-going and well-oiled roller?
>
> (1894:11, cf. 1922:326)

Similarly, Jespersen sees the declensional concord (redundancy) in Latin *opera virorum omnium bonorum veterum* and Old English *ealra godra ealdra manna weorc* as an unwarranted luxury, cf. Modern English *all good old men's works*, asking if 'the phenomena of concord [may not] be survivals from a primitive stage of linguistic development?'. For in 'undeveloped minds we often find a tendency to be more explicit than ... necessary' (1894:38).

Not surprisingly, Jespersen regards the attrition and resulting monosyllabism in Chinese as beneficial to the language as was also the establishment of a fixed word-order, the logical precision of which makes it 'the highest, finest, and accordingly latest developed expedient of speech to which man has attained' (1894:90). It is worth noting that Jespersen did not see fixed word-order as a functional substitution for the loss of flexional endings. On the contrary (and this appears to contradict the *PL* quotation just given), the fixation of word-order *preceded* the loss of endings (1891:50, 1894:96-7). If this had not been the case, the language would for a time have been incomprehensible. Jespersen's view thus comes close to that of the 'functional school' of Horn and Lehnert, cf. Samuels 1972:81.

By why, then, do flexional endings disappear? Jespersen tries to answer this question in relation to the Old English declensional system. He grants that, despite inadequate linguistic records, the presence of Danish vikings may have been of decisive importance as far as the simplificatory processes affecting nominal suffixes are concerned, processes which took place at a particularly early stage in the areas of Danish settlement. On the other hand, he prefers to explain this development, like other changes, on the basis of English itself (1891:98). Again, he advances a 'functional' explanation, attributing the flexional reduction not to the Neogrammarian concept of 'blind' phonetic attrition, but rather to functional inadequacy. In Old English endings like *-a, -e, -u* were in themselves phonetically distinct, but since they were each used in several case-forms and declensional classes, their functional values had become blurred. The effect of this was inconsistency and, eventually, loss. The survival of the Old English *-as* and *-es* endings is due to their greater distinctiveness and clearer functional roles as denotators of plural and genitive (1891:100-104).

Among the developments thought by Jespersen to be indicative of the 'progressive' tendency in English can be mentioned the coalescence of the 2 pers. pron. forms *thou, thee; ye, you* in *you*, whereby English not only acquires more regularity, but also gets rid of the 'useless distinction' between familiar and polite terms of address (1894:276-7, 1938a:223). According to Jespersen (1894:345) it is, in fact, a characteristic of modern languages to have fewer forms than ancient languages (cf. above). Another case in point is the English verb *cut*,

> ... which can serve both as present and past tense, both as singular and plural, both in the first, second and third persons, both in the infinitive, in the imperative, in the indicative, in the subjunctive, and as a past participle ... and remember, moreover, that the identical form, without any inconvenience being occasioned, is also used as a noun (*a cut*) ...
>
> (1894:346, cf. 1922:333)

Jespersen, who calls this example extreme, 'but by no means unique', regards the coalescence of forms and conversion in question as a model of simplicity and economy. I shall deal with *cut* in more detail below and just express a mild surprise at this stage that Jespersen can consider newly formed words like *brood* verb and *breed* noun (from *brood* noun and *breed* verb respectively) an enrichment of the language and at the same time call it 'a positive gain in ease and simplicity' when no new verbs or nouns were created and when one phonetic form just disappeared, cf. Modern English *shroud* noun, verb < Old English *scrūd* noun, but *scrȳdan* verb (1938a:159).

Another example of 'progress' in English is the fact that it has here become grammatically possible to make the indirect object of an active sentence (by Jespersen called 'the real psychological subject') the formal subject of a passive sentence, cf. *I was given permission* .... Logic has here conquered the old grammar (1894:277-8).

Finally, it will be shown how prosody in Jespersen's opinion affected Germanic and therefore English in a 'progressive' way. It is well known that the accent was shifted to the root syllable in Germanic. Jespersen regards this not as a mechanical process as did the Neogrammarians, but as a psychological process: the most important part of the word was stressed, namely the root syllable. By this 'value-stressing' the Germanic system, in comparison with the movable Aryan (i.e. Indo-European) accent,

> ... must be said to be more rational, more logical, as an exact correspondence between the inner and the outer world is established if the most significant element receives the strongest phonetic expression.
>
> (1938a:25)

Germanic gains the further linguistic advantage of having the same syllable (root syllable) stressed in related words so that the connection between them is not obscured as it sometimes is in other Indo-European languages (1938a:23).

Jespersen's investigation of the histories of English and other languages has proved to him that the further back in time we move, the longer and more irregular forms we find. Moreover, the 'clumsy repetitions' (1922:364) of concord increase and so does the irregularity (i.e. the freedom) of word-order. Jespersen has no doubt that, had it been attested 2000 years prior to the earliest inscriptions, Latin (or the ancestor of Latin) would have been vastly more synthetic than even Cicero's language (1894:121, cf. also 1933a:101). To someone (like Jespersen) who, with a phrase borrowed from Ellis, has heard 'the linguistic grass grow', the evolution of human speech represents

> ... a wise natural selection, through which while nearly all innovations of questionable value disappear pretty soon, the

Hans Frede Nielsen

fittest survive and make human speech ever more varied and flexible, and yet ever more easy and convenient to the speakers.

((1905:210) 1938a:198)

Jespersen does not think, however, that any language in the world has yet attained perfection, a state where all irregularity and ambiguity would be banished and the same thing always expressed by the same means (1894:365). But unlike Schleicher, Jespersen thinks that English and Chinese have moved further towards perfection than most languages.

Before we proceed to a brief discussion of the factors that determined Jespersen's view of linguistic evolution, it should be pointed out that Jespersen stuck to his concept of 'progress' in language from 1891, when he became a *dr. phil.*, to his dying day. We can read about it not so much in *MEG*, where he deliberately refrains from propounding a general theory of linguistic change, cf. vol. I, 1909:18 (see however, 1909:v and vol. V, 1940:vi), but in *SEK* (1891), *PL* (1894), *GSEL* (1905), *Language* (1922), *Linguistica* (1933a & c) and *ELC* (1941). There is evidence that the hypothesis may have been conceived even some years before 1891. In his autobiography, *En sprogmands levned* (*SL*), he says (and this was when he sat for one of his written exams for the *cand. mag.* degree at Copenhagen University in the summer of 1887):

Den første opgave i hovedfaget gik ud på sådan noget som en sammenlignende vurdering av latinsk og fransk sprogbygning. Her var jeg rigtig i mit es og fik skrevet en hel del, som måske kan betragtes som en forløber for Fremskridt i sproget.

(1938b:47, cf. also 1938b:68)

III

Above, Jespersen's view of language evolution was depicted as a reaction against Schleicher's linguistic philosophy. It should be noted, however, that Jespersen himself points out that Schleicher is mainly focussed upon because 'he stands out pre-eminently among his contemporaries, and exercises a vast influence down to our day' (1894:4, cf. 1891:3). Among Schleicher's later followers Jespersen mentions specifically Max Müller and Whitney. Paradoxically, both Schleicher and Jespersen professed themselves adherents of Wilhelm von Humboldt, Schleicher in relation to Humboldt's theory of language typology, which Schleicher (wrongly, according to Jespersen (1891:3-4)) construed in a Hegelian manner, and Jespersen with regard to Humboldt's emphasis on language as a means of human communication (cf. above and 1894:13) and the latter's insistence on the *enrichment* of content in the modern languages to counterbalance increasing formal decay (1933a:99-100).

Jespersen was only 17 years old when he was first introduced to the evolutionary theories of Charles Darwin and Herbert Spencer in his freshman year at Copenhagen University. Professor Heegaard, his philosophy teacher, 'taught' (1938b:22) him and his fellow students to admire especially Spencer, and Jespersen readily acknowledges his intellectual debt in this connection (1941:5), a debt which permeates all his written work and particularly, of course, his concept of progress in language. A striking example is the quotation from *GSEL* (1938a:198) cited above: it is no coincidence that it contains Darwinian and Spencerian catch phrases like 'natural selection' and 'the fittest survive', cf. also 1922:297. Not that Jespersen agreed with Spencer in all details, particularly not with the latter's definition of linguistic progress, which was seen to entail an increasing heterogeneity. No, as we are now well aware, Jespersen took progress to be a utilitarian concept meaning 'advance in usefulness', where the ultimate aim would be a language state in which a minimum of effort provided a maximum of linguistic effect (1941:5-7).

It may be asked why Jespersen so stubbornly/faithfully stuck to the same view of language evolution for over 50 years. Perhaps the answer is that his theory was in harmony with his other interests and pursuits in life, indeed with his personality as readers of his autobiography (*SL* 1938b) will no doubt agree, cf. also his predilection for 'virkelighedens fulde dagslys' (1891:66, quoted above) and corresponding distaste for obscure theorizing.

In his obituary of Jespersen, Hammerich (1944) rightly stresses Jespersen's practical turn of mind, which manifested itself in e.g. the pleasure he took in stenography and in finding the shortest possible expressions for things said or conceived. He even introduced abbreviations of his own making into his written work (Hammerich 1944:44-5). As an undergraduate student in Copenhagen, Jespersen had worked as a parliamentary stenographer for several years (1938b:25-7).

It was suggested above (cf. also Jespersen 1891:7, 1894:9 and 1933a:102) that Schleicher had admired classical languages and despised modern ones. In Jespersen's case the reverse appears to hold good: he loved modern languages, especially English, and hated Latin. And it is true of both scholars that their linguistic likes and dislikes can be said to have had bearing on their theories of language evolution. Jespersen's hatred of Latin stemmed from an early age: as a schoolboy he was crammed with Latin six or eight hours every week for seven years. As an undergraduate student in Copenhagen University he worked actively in favour of making Latin, which was the only obligatory subject in the faculty, optional. Jespersen did not succeed then, but managed to achieve his goal about 15 years later when he had become a professor. Later again, in an article in a periodical, he argued against introducing a Danish secondary-school reform in which Latin would come to predominate at the expense of much more important disciplines such as modern languages, cf. 1938b:14, 36, 92, 99. As Professor of English in Copenhagen University he made no secret of what modern language was closest to his heart, cf. 1938b:100.

GSEL can be read as the homage paid by an Anglophile to the English language which is praised for its business-like, virile qualities, its conciseness, logic and sobriety – to say nothing of its noble, rich, pliant and expressive character (1938a:2-16, 234). No wonder that

GSEL became so popular in the English-speaking world and among Anglophiles elsewhere. Schleicher's view of the imperfections of the language were long forgotten.

IV

A final question to be asked: how did Jespersen's theory of language progress fare in the scholarly world? At Jespersen's public defence of his doctoral dissertation in May 1891 (1938b:69), one of the two appointed examiners, Professor Hermann Møller, argued (as many historical linguists would today) in favour of language history moving in spirals (cyclic swings) and not, as Jespersen believed, along a line of constant 'progress' from a starting-point with a maximum of synthesis, cf. above. According to Møller, synthesis was superseded by analysis, which again was replaced by a new synthesis as in the case of the Latin future *amabo*, which in Vulgar Latin was succeeded by a periphrastic future, *amare habeo*, which developed into new synthetic forms in Romance, cf. French *aimerai*, Italian *amerò*. French *aimerai* even seems to be yielding to *je vais aimer*, an analytic expression. Similarly Møller thought that there was a steady alternation between regularity and irregularity in language development (1894:124-5, 1922:424-5, cf. also Møller 1890-92:292-303, Vendryès 1921:420, Samuels 1972:50 and Aitchison 1981:227, 234).

Jespersen countered these and similar attacks by other scholars by saying that regular and analytic forms arise much more frequently than irregular and synthetic ones, which a large-scale, diachronic investigation would confirm (1894:125, 1922:424-5, 1933a:100-101). In *ELC*, Jespersen (1941:7-8) seems to make a concession to his critics by thinking it within the bounds of possibility that

> ... in my endeavour to refute old theories I paid too little attention to those changes that are not beneficial ...

But Jespersen's basic belief in linguistic 'progress' is unchanged:

> ... I still think that I was right in saying that on the whole the average development was progressive and that mankind has benefited by this evolution.

Present-day linguists tend to ignore Jespersen's theory of progress in language development, but hardly because they agree with him! For example, the interest taken in pidgins and creoles within the last few decades have opened up the eyes of linguists to the possibility that so-called normal languages may have their origins in a pidgin-creole process, cf. DeCamp 1971 and Aitchison 1981:192-206, esp. 206. One of the striking characteristics of pidgins is their structural simplicity; in fact, their lack of inflectional suffixes often has the effect that words occur in more than one function or word class, cf. what was said above concerning Modern English *had* and *cut*.

Two recent books on linguistic change that do refer to Jespersen's hypothesis, and which are both at variance with it, are Samuels 1972 and Lass 1980. Samuels's belief that linguistic evolution is a (coincidental) product of parole-based variation, systemic regulation and contact, is clearly incompatible with the concept of a 'teleological drive towards perfection' (1972:50). Lass (1980:133) speaks of Jespersen's 'naive "progressivism" ', an extreme sort of functionalism linked to an evolutionary interpretation of language history. (See also Lass 1980:19-20, 85.) As was pointed out above, Jespersen's concept of language change resembled that of the 'functional school' of Horn and Lehnert. Not surprisingly, Samuels is a severe critic of this school, partly because Horn and Lehnert fail to see the significance of redundancy in grammatical systems and partly because they do not accept the possibility of inflectional loss or weakening through 'sound-law' as proposed by the Neo-grammarians. These points of criticism can easily be levelled at Jespersen's brand of functionalism as well.

It will lead a bit far to go into further detail with the arguments against the functionalists; instead, I refer the reader to Samuels 1972:81-

4 and shall restrict myself to suggesting the existence of an inherent contradiction in Jespersen's hypothesis of language moving towards better speech economy *and* greater communicative efficiency. Surely, a minimum of effort must increase the risk of a breakdown in communication if there is any 'noise in the channel' as there inevitably will be when e.g. interlocutors do not belong to a homogeneous speech community or even speak different dialects. It is an important function of redundancy to ensure that the level of comprehension is maintained despite such 'noise in the channel'. But Jespersen, who nowhere seriously concerns himself with linguistic variation, is not open to the possible function(s) of redundancy. On the contrary, we saw above that Jespersen considered declensional concord an unnecessary luxury indicative of a more primitive language stage. He is right, of course, in thinking that there is little redundancy in Modern English *all good old men's works*, especially as compared with early languages like Latin or Old English (1894:36), but still the level of grammatical redundancy in e.g. Modern English *those girls are my friends/that girl is my friend* is very considerable.

Another case of inconsistency, indeed irony, in Jespersen's view of language change — and this should be seen as an extension of Møller's argument mentioned above — is the assumption that irregularities are at a maximum in the earliest human language and that there has since been a steady movement towards an ideal language, where all irregularity has been done away with, cf. above and 1933a:101, 1922:425-6. It is very ironic that a linguist dedicated to an empirical approach operates with a linguistic utopia, the IDEAL language, in practice ignoring an irrefutable linguistic fact: that there are irregularities in *all* attested languages.

To move to a more specific level of criticism: Jespersen considers the introduction and extended use of the expanded tenses in English an enrichment of the language, a means of expressing 'nice logical distinctions' (*MEG* IV, 1931:213) and 'emotional nuances' (1938a:193). In contrast, the loss of 'distinctions' and 'nuances' in the wake of the demise of the subjunctive in English does not seem to bother Jespersen at all (1938a:194). In other words, complexity is not at odds with Jespersen's concept of progress if it falls within the heading 'enrichment'! (Cf. what was said above concerning newly formed words like *brood* verb and *breed* noun.) Further, Jespersen appears to overlook that the expanded tenses are not only analytic formations, but synthetic ones as well in that they add the suffix *-ing*.

Let me finally return to the verb *cut*, which Jespersen seems to have thought an especially good example of economy at work in the English language. If we look a bit more closely at the quotation from *PL* (1894:346) cited above, it becomes evident that in comparison with other English verbs *cut* is something out of the ordinary in, at most, two respects: (a) it has identical forms in the present (infinitive), preterite and past participle and (b) it is used in the same form as a noun.

As for the former point, *cut* is one of 24 irregular verbs in Modern English with unchanged preterite and past participle forms. Historically, the group derives from Old English weak verbs with short stem vowels followed by *t* or *d* with syncopated medial vowels in the preterite and past participle, e.g. OE *cnyttan, cnytte, gecnytt* which regularly became Modern English *knit, knit, knit,* cf. Old English **cyttan, *cytte, *gecytt* > Modern English *cut, cut, cut. Put, set, shut, slit, wed* also belonged to the group, which was joined by loan verbs from Old Norse (*cast, hit, rid, thrust*), Old French (*cost, hurt, quit*) and Middle Dutch (*split*) and by verbs that were originally strong in Old English (*bid, burst, let, shed*) or which were weak with originally long vowels (*shred, spread, sweat*). *Bet* and *broadcast* joined the group during the Modern English period. (Cf. Hansen & Nielsen 1986:209.)

Jespersen considered the identical present, preterite and past participle forms to be a good example of 'economy in the living tongue'. One may wonder why then only 24 verbs have reached the 'ideal' goal in this respect and if more verbs are on their way towards it. Clearly, the common denominators of the group are their short vowels (*burst* acquired its long /ɜ:/ only in the 18th century), their final *-t* (*-st*) or *-d* and their restricted number of phonemes (three to five with the exception of *broadcast*, but cf. *cast*). In other words, regular sound development and specific phonemic structures are the corner-stones of this group of irregular verbs. It is significant that some of the members of the group have alternative, weak preterite and past participle forms, cf. *knitted, quitted, wedded.* This suggests that identical present, preterite and past participle forms are not a system that is particularly easy to handle. On the contrary, it appears that irregular (strong) verbs have either tended to become regular (weak) or to a large extent (nearly half of all Modern English irregular verbs) ended up on a comparable pattern, i.e. without the usual *-ed* suffix, but with identical preterite and past participle forms and a divergent present (e.g. *stand, stood, stood*).

Unlike Jespersen, I do not regard the identical tense forms of *cut,* etc. as indications of 'progress' in language development, but essentially as examples of inherited raw material exposed to normal phonetic attrition. And I do not think that such forms are preferable in terms of language economy. It is true that forms like *knit, knit, knit* and *cut, cut, cut* have been reduced in consequence of the principle of least effort, but these verbs are *irregular*(!) *minority* forms – in their lack of the preterite/past participle suffix *-ed* as well as in their identical tense forms. Since the general trend of development is towards a present ≠ preterite = past participle pattern, *knit, cut,* etc. are not exactly easy for the speaker to handle as I have already intimated. (Cf. Hansen & Nielsen 1986:232-5.)

As far as the substantival use of *cut* is concerned, the word is not different in this respect from the large majority of the 23 remaining verbs in the group, nor indeed from a great many other English verbs used in substantival functions. No, the only noteworthy thing about *cut* is its membership of an irregular conjugational class, a fact which is of little avail to anybody intent on demonstrating that English is in the process of becoming an ideal language!

Bibliography

Aitchison, J. 1981. *Language Change: Progress or Decay?* London: Fontana.

Baugh, A.C. & T. Cable. 1978. *A History of the English Language.* 3rd ed. London: Routledge & Kegan Paul.

Blake, N.F. & C. Jones (eds.). 1984. *English Historical Linguistics: Studies in Development* (CECTAL Conference Papers Series, No. 3). Sheffield: CECTAL, University of Sheffield.

DeCamp, D. 1971. 'The Study of Pidgin and Creole Languages'. In: D. Hymes (ed.), *Pidginization and Creolization of Languages.* Cambridge: University Press. Pp. 13-39.

Eaton, R., O. Fischer, W. Koopman & F. v.d. Leek (eds.). 1985. *Papers from the 4th International Conference on English Historical Linguistics. Amsterdam, 10-13 April, 1985.* Amsterdam: Benjamins.

Hammerich, L.L. 1944. 'Mindeord over ... Otto Jespersen. 16. Juli 1860 – 30. April 1943. Tale i Videnskabernes Selskabs Møde den 22. Oktober 1943'. *Det Kgl. Danske Videnskabernes Selskab. Oversigt over Selskabets Virksomhed Juni 1943 – Maj 1944.* Copenhagen: Munksgaard. Pp. 41-57.

Hansen, E. & H.F. Nielsen. 1986. *Irregularities in Modern English.* Revised English version. Odense: University Press.

Jespersen, O. 1891. *Studier over engelske kasus.* Copenhagen: Klein.

Jespersen, O. 1894. *Progress in Language with Special Reference to English.* London: Swan Sonnenschein.

Jespersen, O. 1909-49. *A Modern English Grammar on Historical Principles,* I (1909), II (1914), III (1927), IV (1931), V (1940), VI (1942) and VII (1949). London: Allen & Unwin, Copenhagen: Munksgaard.

Jespersen, O. 1922. *Language. Its Nature, Development and Origin.* London: Allen & Unwin.

Jespersen, O. 1933a. 'Energetik der sprache'. (First published in *Scientia* 16 (1914):225ff.) *Linguistica.* Copenhagen: Levin & Munksgaard. Pp. 98-108.

Jespersen, O. 1933b. 'Voiced and Voiceless Fricatives in English'. (Translated and partly rewritten version of final chapter of Jespersen 1891.) *Linguistica*. Copenhagen: Levin & Munksgaard. Pp. 346-83.

Jespersen, O. 1933c. 'Monosyllabism in English'. (Lecture read before the British Academy, 6 Nov., 1928.) *Linguistica*. Copenhagen: Levin & Munksgaard. Pp. 384-408.

Jespersen, O. 1938a. *Growth and Structure of the English Language*. 9th ed. (1st ed. 1905). Leipzig: Teubner.

Jespersen, O. 1938b. *En sprogmands levned*. Copenhagen: Gyldendal.

Jespersen, O. 1941. *Efficiency in Linguistic Change*. (Det Kgl. Danske Videnskabernes Selskab. Historisk-filologiske Meddelelser. 47, 4.) Copenhagen: Munksgaard.

Lass, R. 1980. *On Explaining Language Change*. Cambridge: University Press.

Luick, K. 1921-40. *Historische Grammatik der englischen Sprache*, I,1 - I,2. Leipzig: Tauchnitz.

Møller, H. 1890-92. Review of Jespersen 1891. In: *Nordisk Tidskrift for Filologi* (ny Række) 10:292-317.

Mustanoja, T. 1960. *A Middle English Syntax*, I. Helsinki: Mémoires de la Société Néophilologique.

Pyles, T. & J. Algeo. 1982. *The Origins and Development of the English Language*. 3rd ed. New York: Harcourt Brace Jovanovich.

Rydén, M. 1979. *An Introduction to the Historical Study of English Syntax*. Stockholm: Almqvist & Wiksell.

Samuels, M.L. 1972. *Linguistic Evolution with Special Reference to English*. Cambridge: University Press.

Schibsbye, K. 1972. *Origin and Development of the English Language*, I. Copenhagen: Nordisk Sprog- og Kulturforlag.

Schleicher, A. 1869. *Die Deutsche Sprache*. 2. Aufl. Stuttgart: Cotta.

Strang, B.M.H. 1970. *A History of English*. London: Methuen.

Vendryès, J. 1921. *Le Langage*. Paris: La Renaissance du Livre.

Visser, F.T. 1963-73. *An Historical Syntax of the English Language*, I-III. Leiden: Brill.

Hans Frede Nielsen

Acknowledgements: I would like to thank Erik W. Hansen, Arne Juul, Fritz Larsen, Povl Skårup and Palle Spore for their comments on this paper.

78

W. Nelson Francis

OTTO JESPERSEN AS GRAMMARIAN

Jespersen as a theoretical grammarian

Otto Jespersen is best known, certainly, as a practicing grammarian, as evidenced above all in his major work, the *Modern English Grammar*. But he was also a theoretician. In fact, even as he was working on the *MEG*, he was formulating, developing, and eventually publishing a remarkably full theory of grammar which supplied the foundation for his detailed expository and pedagogical grammars. This theory is most fully described and argued in two books both published while the *MEG* was in progress: *The Philosophy of Grammar* (*PG*, 1924) and *Analytic Syntax* (*AS*, 1937). The former is a full discursive treatment; the latter, which he considered a 'kind of supplement' to it, is a formulaic treatment of hundreds of constructions, mostly but not exclusively English, according to a system of his own devising, with extensive explanatory and justificatory comments. Between them, these two books set forth the most extensive and original theory of universal grammar prior to the work of Chomsky and other generative grammarians of the last thirty years. In them Jespersen puts forward many new ideas which have been variously treated by succeeding grammarians – some accepted, often silently, and included with or without attribution in later work; others rejected or simply ignored. The same may be said of his terminology: some of his inventions, such as *quantifier, mass-word*, and *existential sentence*, have become standard, while others like *dramatic present* and *plural of approximation* have not.

The title *The Philosophy of Grammar* seems to indicate Jespersen's belief in the existence of a generalized abstraction, *grammar*, distinct from and superordinate to the grammars of individual languages.

This concept of universal grammar was popular in the eighteenth century, became discredited as a result of the study of many 'exotic' languages in the nineteenth and earlier twentieth centuries, and has been restored to favor in the syntactic theories of the 1970s and 1980s. Jespersen raises the question of the existence of a universal grammar early in *PG* and devotes four pages to discussing it (47-50). At this point he seems to support the conclusion of Steinthal, which he quotes:

> 'A universal grammar is no more conceivable than a universal form of political Constitution or of religion, or than a universal plant or animal form'.
>
> *(PG: 48)*

But he does not categorically adopt this position. He goes on to quote C. Alphonso Smith, who states that 'One comes almost to believe that the norms of syntax are indestructible, so persistently do they reappear in unexpected places' (*PG*: 48).

In his concluding chapter, in a final section entitled 'The Soul of Grammar', Jespersen indeed comes as near as his cautious nature will allow to an acceptance of grammatical universals, if not of an overall universal grammar. As he looks back over his work, he concludes:

> My endeavour has been, without neglecting investigation into the details of the languages known to me, to give due prominence to the great principles underlying the grammars of all languages, and thus to make my contribution to a grammatical science based at the same time on sound psychology, on sane logic, and on solid facts of linguistic history.
>
> *(PG: 344)*

It is characteristic that although he professes to have dealt with 'the great principles underlying the grammars of all languages', he is careful to make clear that his conclusions are based on 'the details of the languages known to me'. It is apparent from the illustrations used not only in *PG* but also in *AS* that these languages are Danish, English, German, Dutch, Latin, French, Spanish, Italian, and Greek, as well as the older Germanic languages Old English, Old Norse, Icelandic, and Gothic – all Indo-European, it will be noted. But he also uses examples, citing his secondary sources, from Finno-Ugric, Hungarian, Finnish, Russian, Sanskrit, Chinese, and Greenlandic. The focus is obviously on European culture languages. The vast fields of African, Amerindian, Oceanic, Oriental, and Australian languages were unknown to him; in fact, a great deal of the research and study in these areas has taken place since he wrote.

Jespersen's grammatical theory is based on three concepts, to a considerable degree original with him. These are *rank, junction,* and *nexus*. He came to believe that all syntactic constructions can be explained in terms of these three ideas, which are fully dealt with in *PG* and *AS*, and form the basis of his work as a practical grammarian, especially in the later volumes of *MEG*.

In Jespersen's view, individual words may be classified in two ways. The first is the traditional semantic classification into *parts of speech*. He adopts the usual categories, except that he lumps together adverbs, prepositions, and conjunctions as *particles*. 'This fifth class [in addition to substantives, adjectives, pronouns, and verbs] may be negatively characterized as made up of all those words that cannot find any place in any of the first four classes' (*PG*: 91). This classification is of the individual words in themselves, so that they can be labeled in a dictionary. The second classification, that of *rank*, is based on the functions of words in syntactic constructions. He distinguishes three levels or ranks, though he admits that there can be more, of diminishing importance. A word which we have come to call the *head* of a construction, he calls a *primary*. Words immediately dependent upon the primaries are *secondaries*, which may have *tertiaries* dependent on them. Thus a noun phrase such as *extremely hot weather* has the noun *weather* as primary, the adjective *hot* as secondary, and the adverb *extremely* as tertiary. The distinction between word-class classification and rank classification is that the former remains constant while the latter varies with the syntactic structure involved. Thus while *weather* is always a noun (except in nautical usage, where it may be a verb), it is not always a primary, as in *weather report*, where it is a secondary dependent on the primary *report*. This distinction allows a clear cut solution to the problem of expressions such as *the poor are always with us* or *a word to the wise*, which traditional grammar solved by calling *poor* and *wise* adjectives used as nouns and structural grammarians called pure nouns marked as such by the definite article and function as subject or object of a preposition. For Jespersen they are simply adjectives used as primaries.

Jespersen extends the concept of rank to a general class of *word groups*, which includes all structures of more than one word which serve a unitary syntactic function – noun phrases, prepositional phrases, relative and complement clauses, adverbial clauses. Thus in the example *the weather report is favorable* he would call the group *weather report* a primary because of its function as subject, but would further analyze it into two nouns, the first a secondary and the second a primary. In the system of notation in *AS* the sentence would be S (2 1) V P (2). A separate notation with a hyphen, S (2-1) would be used if the word group is considered a compound word. Jespersen admits the difficulty of making this distinction in his discussion of *Word* in *PG* (93-95). But since this distinction does not affect the syntactic function of the word group and its components, this is a lexicographic more than a syntactic problem. A given collocation of words such as *weather report* may serve the same function – in this case subject – regardless of whether it is a phrase or a compound.

When the concept of rank is extended to word groups as large as clauses, the notation may become quite complicated. Take, for example, a sentence which Jespersen gives in both English and German, with the same notational analysis (*AS*: 65):

Heine, whose poems you admire, was a German Jew.

Heine, dessen gedichte Sie bewundern, war ein deutscher jude.

This is analyzed as:

$$\text{S} \ (1 \ 2 \ (\text{O} \ (1^{2c} \ 1) \ \text{S}_2 \ \text{V})) \ \text{V} \ \text{P} \ (2 \ 1)$$

This can be interpreted as saying: The overall construction is a sentence (predication) beginning with a subject consisting of a primary [noun] modified by a following secondary [relative clause] which begins with a word group as object, consisting of a primary modified by a primary serving as both a secondary and a connective, followed by a new subject and a finite verb. The main sentence continues with a finite verb and a predicative consisting of a secondary modifying a primary. As we shall see later in the discussion of *AS*, the capitals indicate major syntactic categories and the parentheses following give the constituents of each. The resulting bracketing calls to mind the constituent analysis of structural and later generative grammar; it can even be resolved into a kind of tree:

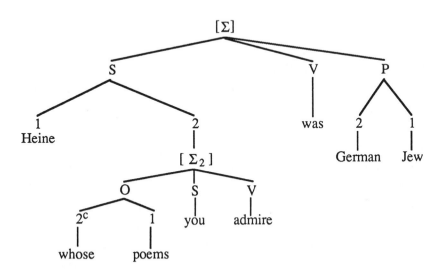

The concept of rank is thus basically notational, setting up a hierarchy of relational categories distinct from the semantic hierarchy of parts of speech. It is particularly useful in the resolution of problems in an analytical language in which morphology is sparse and words may shift function without formal notice – English, par excellence. In a highly synthetic language, it is likely to be the case that nouns are always primaries, adjectives and finite verbs secondaries, and adverbs tertiaries. If so, the concept of rank is redundant. In fact, the traditional 'universal grammar' of the eighteenth century is inherited from such languages, Latin and Greek, which accounts for its heavy dependence on the 'part of speech' classification. But as we have seen, in a language such as English, a (semantic) adjective can be a (syntactic) primary (*the poor are always with us*) and a noun can be a secondary (*weather report*).

It is hard to see how the rank concept could be applied at all to polysynthetic languages like many American Indian languages, where a single 'word' may contain a cluster of relational units. On the other hand, it might be quite useful in analyzing so-called isolating languages like Chinese or Viet Namese. Unfortunately, Jespersen knew little about these; polyglot though he was, the many languages he knew were all of the late Indo-European pattern, in which original synthetic complexity had given way to more or less complete analyticity. One wonders if he would have developed the rank concept if his favorite language for study had been other than English.

Rank, then, is a rather secondary notion. But the other two concepts, *junction* and *nexus*, are at the heart of Jespersen's syntactic theory. Every genuine syntactic construction can be classed as one or the other; between them they account for all of syntax. Jespersen devotes considerable space in *PG* to making clear the distinction between them. He begins with the pair of expressions *the furiously barking dog* and *the dog barks furiously*. He points out that these two word groups express the same idea, and that the component words have the same rank in each: *dog* is a primary, *barks* and *barking* are secondaries, and *furiously* is a tertiary. 'Yet there is a fundamental difference between them ...: we shall call the former kind *junction* and the latter *nexus*' (*PG*: 97). He goes on to attempt to describe this fundamental difference:

> In a junction a secondary element (an adjunct) is joined to a primary word as a label or distinguishing mark: ... Adjunct and primary together form *one* denomination, a composite name for what might just as well be called by a single name....
>
> A nexus, on the contrary, always contains two ideas which must necessarily remain separate: the secondary term adds something new to what has already been named.
>
> (*PG*: 115f)

This could be summarized as saying that a junction describes or particularizes a referent, while a nexus asserts an action, process, or state (though Jespersen does not make this threefold division in these terms).

Jespersen devotes three important chapters of *PG* (VIII-X) to elaborating these two key concepts. Junction is relatively simple. One important aspect is the familiar distinction between *restrictive* and *non-restrictive* adjuncts. A paradox connected with the former is that while substantives are more restricted in meaning than adjectives (as Jespersen had contended in his discussion of word-classes), the adjunction of a qualifying adjective to a substantive creates a more restricted total meaning. His example is *a red rose*, in which the more specific substantive *rose* is further narrowed in significance by the very general adjective *red*. On the other hand, a non-restrictive adjunct does not further limit the reference of the substantive but simply further characterizes it. The extreme case is when the ultimately specific substantive, a proper name, is modifed by one or more adjuncts, as in *Beautiful Evelyn Hope is dead* or French *le bon Dieu*. In addition to adjectives, Jespersen deals perceptively with appositives, genitives, demonstratives, articles, and relative clauses, each of which type of adjunct may be either restrictive or non-restrictive.

The concept of nexus is more complex and more difficult. While junction is based on the relatively simple notion of modification, nexus cannot in the same way be considered simply another name for predication. It is true that the most developed form of nexus contains a finite verb, yet Jespersen admits several types of nexus in which either the verb is missing (*understood* is the old-fashioned term; the modern generative grammarian refers to *deletion*) or there is no verb at all, expressed or understood. The basic distinction is ultimately semantic. As we have already seen, the parts of a junction are constituents of a larger structure which belongs to the same word-class as the primary which is its head, while the basic parts of a nexus combine to form a new type of structure which is both semantically and syntactically different from either (or any) of its components. Jespersen struggles with various metaphors to express this distinction: 'Whereas the junction is more stiff and rigid, the nexus is more pliable; it is, as it were, animated or articulate.... A junction is like a picture, a nexus like a process or a drama' (*PG*: 116). The nexus 'has life in it' (*PG*: 115).

Jespersen claims originality not only for the term but for the association in the class of nexuses of a hierarchy of constructions which the older grammarians had treated separately. This hierarchy is most clearly described in *AS* (122):

> The life-giving power [of nexus] is found in the highest degree in the finite verb,... It is found in a lesser degree in infinitives, gerunds, nexus-substantives and agent-nouns, and these four may be said to form a decreasing scale, in which the life-giving power is more and more diminished.

Jespersen develops this classification in some detail in chapters IX and X of *PG*. He covers the finite verb only briefly, presumably because of its familiar treatment as the center of predications in standard grammars. He goes on to discuss infinitives and gerunds, both of which he considers to have originated as deverbal substantives. Infinitives 'have approached the finite verbs morphologically and syntactically' (*PG*: 140) in such functions as taking objects, forming junctions with negatives and adverbs, developing tense and voice distinctions, and in some languages taking nominative subjects. Gerunds, like the English *-ing* forms, have suffered a development 'by which what was originally a pure substantive

86

formed only from some particular verb comes to be formed from any verb and acquires more and more of the characteristics of the finite verb' (*PG*: 140). He discusses briefly the vexed point of English grammatical usage in which the subject of the gerund, originally always genitive, has come to be frequently in the 'common case' of nouns or even the nominative of pronouns. All these developments allow these forms to take the place, as what are now called *minor clauses*, of complement clauses with finite verbs.

Jespersen also discusses at some length various types of nexus without a verb. Among these are nominal sentences – in English consisting of a predicative followed by a noun, the whole being semantically different from a junction, as in *funny fellow, Mr. Jones*. Others are the double object or object complement construction, which Jespersen calls *nexus-object*, as in *we elected him president*, and the absolute construction (Jespersen's *nexus subjunct*), as in *the business concluded, the meeting adjourned*.

One of the more interesting aspects of Jespersen's concept of nexus is his identifying of a class of nouns he calls *nexus-substantives*. These are of two types: deverbal nouns like *arrival, departure, movement, sleep*, etc., and de-adjectival nouns like *cleverness, rapidity, accuracy,* etc. Jespersen points out that these are parallel and semantically equivalent to assertions with finite verbs, as in *the doctor's arrival = the doctor arrived*. In his analysis the original verb, a secondary, becomes the primary, and the original primary subject becomes a secondary in the genitive. He still considers the construction to be a nexus rather than a junction. Finally he cites examples of one-member nexus, in which the primary (subject) is unexpressed but 'present in the mind', as in *to know her is to love her, he likes to travel (traveling)*. This is one of the few times that he calls on an understood or elliptical element to complete a construction. It is necessary here to support his contention that a nexus must have a subject (in *AS*: 128 he modifies this to the extent of interpreting Latin *pluit*, 'it is raining', as a true subjectless nexus). I leave it to modern grammarians to relate Jespersen's insights here to the generative concepts of *raising* and *equi*.

87

The remainder of Jespersen's grammatical theorizing is more traditional. But he is always consistent, at least in his later work, in finding a solution to any grammatical problem in terms of his three principles of rank, junction and nexus. This is most notably illustrated in *Analytic Syntax*, which Jespersen considers 'the crowning effort of many years' occupation with grammatical problems [which] thus forms a kind of supplement to my "Philosophy of Grammar"' (*AS*: ix). It is admirable in both these respects. As a 'crowning effort' it applies his mature grammatical thought to hundreds of sentences and expressions in a dozen or so languages, and as a supplement to *PG* it supplies a wide variety of illustrative citations for that theoretical work, which is rather sparing in its use of examples. It may also be considered a kind of calculus which, by insisting on objective assignment and handling of a handful of symbols, leads to clear solutions of grammatical problems. Jespersen even compares his symbology to 'the wonderful system of symbols which during the last few centuries has contributed so much to make mathematics (and in some degree logic) exact and more easy to manage than was possible with the unwieldy word-descriptions used formerly. My system aims at providing linguists with some of the same advantages' (*AS*: 3). But he hastens to point out that his system cannot have the same universality as those of mathematics and chemistry because of the social conditioning of language, which leads to variation in the solution of linguistic necessities far greater than is permitted in those more exact sciences. Here he once again touches the question of universal grammar and settles for the compromise position: there are many grammatical universals but no single monolithic universal grammar.

Jespersen's system is relatively simple, consisting of a collection of symbols – mostly capital or lower case letters – which are placed in a string following exactly the surface structure of a sentence or other construction. In this respect it resembles the system later devised by Fries (1952) and differs from those of Reed and Kellogg diagrams or the bracketed strings and trees of various forms of generative grammar, where the symbols (or, in the case of Reed and Kellogg, words) are deployed to indicate the underlying, logical, or deep structure. This close adherence to surface order created a few problems, notably with discontinuous constituents such as complex tense forms and phrasal verbs. As we shall see, Jespersen found solutions for these.

The principal set of symbols includes twelve capital letters, seven of which stand for grammatical relations: S for subject, V for finite verb, O and *O* for direct and indirect object, etc. Among the others are I for infinitive, G for gerund, and Y for 'agent-substantive or participle'. The lower case letters stand for minor categories: p for preposition, s for 'lesser' or dummy subjects, etc. A third set consists of the rank numbers, which are used to indicate the constituents of the major categories; thus S (2 1) denotes a subject realized by a phrase consisting of a primary modified by a secondary, e.g. *a tall man* (Jespersen's system disregards articles). In addition to these three sets, there are various superscripts specifying grammatical relations: ^{n} for negation, ^{c} for connective, etc.; and various types of brackets (we have seen the use of parentheses to specify constituents): square brackets for appositives and extrapositives, curly brackets for single lexemes which incorporate two or more grammatical relations, as {SV} for Latin *amo*, which includes both subject and verb. The repertory of symbols, 47 in all, is completed by various miscellaneous characters such as & for coordinators, + for adjective-noun compounds, etc. The way the system works is best shown by a few of the more complex examples.

What money I have is at your disposal.
S (O (2^c 1) S$_2$ V) V P (pl (1^2 X))

This can be paraphrased as saying:
1. The whole is a sentence, consisting of subject, finite verb, and predicative – S V P
2. The subject is a clause, consisting of object, a different subject, and a finite verb – O S$_2$ V
3. The object of this clause is a phrase consisting of a primary modified by a secondary with connective function [*what*] – 2^c 1

4. The predicative of the main sentence is a prepositional phrase with a primary as object – pl

5. This object consists of a nexus-substantive [*disposal*] modified by a primary serving as a secondary (i.e. a possessive pronoun) – 1^2 X

Wir lachten, als wir ihn laufen sahen.
S V 3 (3^c S O (S_2 I) V)

paraphrased as:

1. The sentence consists of a subject, verb, and adverbial (tertiary) clause – S V 3

2. The clause consists of a tertiary connective [*als*], a subject, object, and verb – 3^c S O V

3. The subject of the clause is the same as the subject of the main sentence (no subscript on the second S)

4. The object in the clause is an infinitive phrase consisting of an infinitive with a different subject – S_{2*} I

Det ærgrer mig at jeg ikke kan komme.
s V O S (3^c S_2 3^n V)

paraphrased as:

1. The sentence has a dummy subject standing for the true subject, which is extraposed; also an object and a finite verb.

2. The true subject is a complement clause introduced by a tertiary connective – 3^c [*at*]

3. This clause has its own subject, a negative particle, and a verb. (Nothing indicates that the subject of this clause is coreferential with the object of the main clause or that both of them are pronouns.)

I don't know the man Mary is talking to.
S V^n O ($1*$ 2 (S_2 V $p*$))   or
S V^n O (O_2* 2 (S_2 W$*$))

Both of these analyses use asterisks to indicate that two elements, separately located, form a single constituent. In the first analysis, the relative clause is interpreted as showing preposition stranding, with *to* separated from its object *man*. In the second analysis, *talk to* is interpreted as a phrasal verb (symbol W) separated from its front-shifted object. In the Comment section of *AS*, Jespersen mentions a third possibility with this type of what he calls 'contact clauses', which is to posit 'a non-existent relative pronoun'. But he prefers the other two analyses, not only because on the whole he avoids zero constituents but also because he believes they are more in conformity with the natural feeling that, in this case, *man* 'is felt as belonging to what follows as well as what precedes' (*AS*: 151), i.e. it is object both of the main verb *know* and also of the clausal verb *is talking to*.

Although Jespersen normally treats complex verb forms as single ranked units (usually rank 2), there is a problem when two or more parts of the verb are separated, either by an adverb or by inversion of the first auxiliary with the subject. His solution is to designate the separated auxiliary by lower-case v, which stands for 'lesser' verbs. Thus

> Has he come?
> Est-il venu?
> Ist er gekommen?

are all coded v S V

In spite of its obvious versatility and flexibility, Jespersen's system has some serious defects. One of these certainly is its failure to identify the word-classes to which grammatical elements belong, with the exception of finite verb, infinitive, gerund, and preposition. This is in line with his frequently expressed view that 'part of speech' distinctions are not grammatical but semantic and thus should not play a part in syntactic analysis. Here there is a sharp contrast between Jespersen's analysis and that of early generative grammar such as Chomsky's Standard Theory (Chomsky 1965). Jespersen bases all on syntactic relations such as subject, object, adjunct, which are variously filled by different types of words depending on the meaning. The generative grammarians worked directly with part of speech designations like N, NP, VP, etc., deriving elements such as subject from position in the string or tree – e.g. subject as the only NP directly dominated by S. Jespersen's system is more like recent syntactic theories such as Relational Grammar.

Another deficiency in Jespersen's system is the omission of many features which other grammars see fit to include. In the Comment section of *AS* he gives a list of these, under the heading 'What not Symbolized': number, person, tense, and gender (*AS*: 94). To which might be added aspect and mode. All of these are discussed in *PG*, but receive no symbolic recognition in *AS*. Thus all finite verbs (except the split constituent ones) are lumped together under V, all adjectives are 2 when they modify a noun, and so on. This means that significant syntactic features like anaphora and concord are not registered. A chapter on Case in the comment section describes at some length the case systems of Latin and Finnish, but comes to the conclusion that 'it is impossible in a system like ours to find any place for cases' (*AS*: 108). It is not that Jespersen does not believe that these matters are important – in fact, he discusses them at considerable length in *PG* – only that in an austerely functional system like that of *AS* there is no place for distinctions based on form or semantics, no matter how they may influence syntax. It is no doubt these deficiencies in the system which has kept it from being taken up by other grammarians. It was, in effect, stillborn.

Jespersen as practical grammarian

Throughout his career, Jespersen wrote grammars – whole grammars and fragments of grammars, pedagogical and descriptive grammars. The earliest was a pedagogical grammar published in 1885, while he was still an undergraduate: *Kortfattet engelsk Grammatik for Tale- og Skriftsproget* ('A Short Grammar of Spoken and Written English'). Six years later he wrote as his doctoral dissertation *Studier over engelske kasus*

('Studies on Case in English'). Ten years after that, two years after his appointment to the chair of English at Copenhagen, he published a primer of English: *Engelsk Begynderbog*. His bibliography shows many articles, long and short, on such topics as *Negation in English and Other Languages* (1917), *Notes on Relative Clauses* (1926), *The Expanded Tenses* (1931). Much of the material in these papers, many of them published in the British series of the Society for Pure English, was later incorporated into the *Modern English Grammar*. In fact, they often seem to be by-products of his work on that great compendium. He was, of course, not exclusively engaged with grammar during this period. He was also concerned with language pedagogy, English phonology, and the history of English, as is shown in the chapters of this book by Knud Sørensen, Jørgen Rischel, Hans Frede Nielsen, and Jørgen Erik Nielsen.

There is not room here to give attention to all of these studies, important though they are. Instead I should like to confine my discussion to his two best-known works, the seven-volume *Modern English Grammar on Historical Principles* and the much shorter *Essentials of English Grammar (EEG)*. If he had written nothing else in his long career, these would have been enough to establish him as a linguist and Anglist of the highest order.

The *Modern English Grammar* (henceforth *MEG*) was indeed a life work. The first of the seven volumes was published in 1909 and the last was published forty years later. During this period Jespersen worked at it sporadically, with interruptions of varying length occasioned by work on other books, two World Wars (during the second of which his native country was occupied by enemy forces), and an extended stay in America. But whether actually writing or not, he continued to collect voluminous files of citations from his extensive reading, a collection which was the source of the rich store of illustrative examples which is one of the outstanding features of the work. It is clear from these citations, as also from the title of the book, that his model was the *New English Dictionary on Historical Principles*, which was still coming out volume by volume during the first twenty years of Jespersen's work. He frequently acknowledges his debt to the *OED* in his prefaces, and though he never expressly says so, it is clear that he intended to produce a grammatical counterpart to Murray's lexicographical masterpiece.

One thing that strikes the reader who first approaches the *MEG* is the unusual arrangement of the material. Jespersen begins traditionally with a volume on *Sounds and Spellings*. But then, instead of dealing next with morphology, he goes directly to syntax, thoroughly dealt with in four volumes which appeared over a period of 27 years. He finally comes to morphology in Part VI, which was based on old notes and collections, and in which he was assisted by three of his former students. The whole is completed by another volume simply called *Syntax*, as though the four volumes of *Syntax I-IV* did not exist. A good deal of this last volume was written by Jespersen's student and colleague Niels Haislund, who also revised the portions which Jespersen had written before his death in 1943.

Jespersen explains in rather ingratiating fashion in the Preface to part II (*Syntax*, vol. 1) the reasons for his departure from traditional order:

> It was originally my plan after the first volume of this work, which deals with sounds and spellings, to go on to Morphology and finally to Syntax.... My reasons for now deviating from this order and bringing out the syntactical before the morphological part, are partly of a purely personal character. When I took up work again after a rest necessitated by overstrain during a nine months' stay in America, I wanted something pleasurable to do and thought Syntax more attractive than Morphology;... Besides I was told by friends here and abroad that they were especially eager to see my treatment of Syntax, and I felt that I had perhaps more new and original points of view to offer here than in pure Morphology.
>
> (*MEG*: II.v)

This is a very honest statement. The Morphology volume, when it finally came out in 1942, is the most traditional and least original part of the work. During the period between the wars, Jespersen's mind was very much on syntax. Even as he was working on the four syntactic volumes of *MEG*, he was developing the theoretical views expressed in *PG* and *AS*, which have been discussed above. When he finally took up morphology in the late 30s, he was content to delegate the major part of the work to Haislund and two other 'young philologists', Paul Christophersen and Knud Schibsbye, to whom he handed over the notes from his morphology lectures of 1925 as well as his extensive citations and notes. He did, however, keep in close touch with them and subjected their work to close revision before publication.

The final volume of *MEG*, Part VII, is simply entitled *Syntax*, as noted above. It is not easy to understand its relationship to the rest of the work. In the Preface to the *Morphology* volume, Jespersen refers to it as 'the final part of the Syntax, of which a few chapters have already been written' (*MEG* VI:viii). Only six of eighteen chapters are exclusively Jespersen's work. The rest was done by Haislund, based on earlier notes and drafts by Jespersen, and read by him before publication. The material of the volume is of two kinds: review and expansion of material covered earlier in Parts II-V, and some new topics, such as Case and Mood, not previously dealt with. There is thus a great deal of back reference to the earlier volumes, mixed with new analysis and illustration. The user looking for Jespersen's (and his collaborators') views on many topics often must locate the treatment in two places – once in one of the earlier four volumes and once in Part VII. For example, in the case of indefinite relative clauses (now commonly called *free relatives*) there is an extended discussion in chapter 3 of Part III, dealing especially with pronoun forms and syntactic functions of the clauses, and a further discussion in chapter 18 of Part VII dealing with the mood of the verb. The same kind of division is found with such important features as quantifiers, articles, and other deictics, which are dealt with in Part II and again, usually at greater length, in Part VII. In these cases it looks as though, writing thirty years later, Jespersen had reached more mature conclusions which, had he lived, might have been incorporated into a thorough revision of the older parts of the work.

Though somewhat confusing to the reader, this state of affairs is interesting as a record of Jespersen's change and growth through nearly half a century of thinking about grammar. Unfortunately the complete work is not sufficiently equipped with guideposts for the occasional user. After all, it is a reference grammar rather than a single coherent and connected study. Only the most dedicated grammarian would sit down to read it through. But many students of English have used it to cast light on some point of English grammar and many still do. I for one have frequently had the experience of hitting upon what I thought was an original idea, only to find on checking that Jespersen had been there before me. This process of checking would be easier if more help in tracking down relevant passages were available. Specifically, though each volume is competently indexed, there is no overall index to the whole. So unless one is thoroughly familiar with the organization of the material, he may have to look through several indices and tables of contents to find what he is looking for. It would even have helped if the several syntax volumes had been given subtitles, briefly listing the contents of each. Subtitles of this sort would direct the user to the right volume, whose detailed table of contents and index would lead him to the relevant sections.

But these are minor considerations. *MEG* remains a master-work, which will continue to be consulted in spite of the appearance of more modern reference grammars such as that of Quirk et al. (1985). Its great virtues, in addition to the profusion of illustrative citations, are originality and perceptiveness of approach and modesty and clarity of style. Few grammar books make such good reading.

As we have seen, the production of *MEG* extended over virtually all of Jespersen's scholarly career, from the phonology volume in 1909 to the posthumous final syntax volume. He was, of course, engaged in other projects during this time. The first volume of *Syntax* came out in 1913, on the eve of World War I, and the second not until 1927. But this period was an especially productive one, since it saw the publication of three major works: *Language* (1922), *Philosophy of Grammar* (1924), and *Mankind, Nature, and Individual from a Linguistic Point of View*

(1925). The third volume of *Syntax* appeared in 1931, and the fourth, after another interval, in 1940. This, too, was a productive period, during which Jespersen produced, in addition to many articles and lectures, two important grammatical works: *Analytic Syntax* (1937) which we have already discussed, and what is arguably his most familiar and popular book, *Essentials of English Grammar* (1933). The two decades between the wars thus saw not only steady progress with *MEG*, but the maturation of Jespersen's theoretical views on grammar and their application to the writing of practical grammars, both pedagogical and reference. *EEG* is thus both a model compendium of grammatical information and a remarkable illustration of the working out of a coherent and consistent grammatical system, firmly established on a body of general theory. As such it can be considered an epitome of Jespersen's work as theoretical and practical grammarian.

The most important part of Jespersen's grammatical theory which first appears in *EEG* is the concept of nexus. This is nowhere dealt with in the first three Syntax volumes of *MEG*. It received theoretical development, as we have seen, in *PG*. In *EEG* it is introduced early, along with Jespersen's other main concept, that of rank. And it dominated the treatment of nexus-substantives, gerunds, and infinitives toward the end of the book. This section is a kind of forecast of the fourth Syntax volume of *MEG*, which is wholly devoted to nexus and contains eleven chapters, nearly 200 pages, on infinitives. This is one of the most complex areas of English grammar, and remains one of Jespersen's most distinguished accomplishments as a grammarian.

There are other good things in *EEG*. The discussion of time and tense, including extended treatment of *will, shall, would,* and *should,* in essence a summary of the fuller treatment which occupies the whole of Syntax III of *MEG*, is clear and perceptive. Here, however, the modern reader finds two things lacking: treatment of the other modal auxiliaries and of the modals as a class, and distinction between tense and aspect. Jespersen treats the English perfect and progressive (which he calls 'the expanded tense') simply as tenses, though his statement of their meanings sounds more like what modern grammarians call aspect. For example, he says of the perfect:

> ...the Perfect is a retrospective present, which connects a past occurrence with the present time, either as continued up to the present moment... or as having results and consequences bearing on the present moment.
>
> (*EEG*: 243)

And of the progressive:

> The chief use of the expanded tenses is to serve as a frame round something else, which may or may not be expressly indicated.... If we say *he was (on) hunting*, we mean that the hunting (which may be completed now) had begun, but was not completed at the time mentioned or implied in the sentence; this element of relative incompletion is very important if we want to understand the expanded tenses, even if it is not equally manifest in all cases.
>
> (*EEG*: 263)

These two discussions remind us of Twaddell's more concise definitions: 'current relevance' for the perfect and 'limited duration' for the progressive. (Twaddell 1963)

Jespersen's failure to use the term *aspect* for these verb forms is not a matter of ignorance. In *PG* he has four pages on aspect, which he calls 'a subject which has been very warmly discussed in recent decades', a statement which he reinforces by a footnote citing eleven references, mostly to German grammarians (*PG*: 286-89). He finds the discussion confused and inconsistent, and gives his own set of seven notional categories which seem to belong in this discussion, though he 'expressly' says that 'the different phenomena which others have brought together under this one class ... should not from a purely notional point of view be classed together' (*PG*: 287). It is undoubtedly this perceived vagueness of the term which leads him to avoid its use in English grammars.

The discussion of *will* and *shall* both in *EEG* and *MEG* Syntax IV is refreshing, not only in its avoidance of the simplistic prescriptions of so many grammars deriving from eighteenth century grammars, but also in its perception of the semantic problem underlying the variability and uncertainty of usage. The problem, as Jespersen sees it, is that there are only two auxiliaries to express three notions: volition, obligation, and futurity. He seems to suggest that the solution may be seen in the increasing use of *have to* for obligation and *going to* for futurity, leaving *will* for volition. The increasing frequency of these two quasi-auxiliaries, in addition to *used to* for the habitual past, bears out the accuracy of his perception.

There is much more to be said about these two great grammars, but limitation of space prevents. In sum we may conclude that though some of Jespersen's theoretical ideas have been superseded and some have never caught on with others, these two books remain as monuments to a great grammarian, whose theory and practice can still be stimulating to a modern student of English grammar.

References

Books by Otto Jespersen are not listed here. Their titles and dates are given in the text.

Chomsky, N. 1965. *Aspects of the Theory of Syntax*. Cambridge, Mass.: M.I.T. Press.
Fries, C. 1952. *The Structure of English: An Introduction to the Construction of English Sentences*. New York: Harcourt, Brace.
Quirk, R., S. Greenbaum, G. Leech & J. Svartvik. 1985. *A Comprehensive Grammar of the English Language*. London & New York: Longman.
Twaddell, W.F. 1963. *The English Verb Auxiliaries*. 2nd edition revised. Providence: Brown University Press.

Fritz Larsen

JESPERSEN'S NEW INTERNATIONAL AUXILIARY LANGUAGE

Some readers will no doubt find that this chapter calls for an apology. They may have little sympathy for the idea of an artificial[1] language as such, or they may consider Jespersen's work in this area a regrettable parenthesis in his scholarly career and his creation of yet another language the crowning folly.

No apology will be offered. It is true that towards the end of his life Jespersen expressed some qualms about the time and energy he had invested in these projects, but he did devote no less than two chapters of his autobiography to them. His interest in the matter covered practically his whole life, from his rejection of Volapük in his student days to suggested reforms in his own creation Novial a few years before his death.

It is no surprise that Jespersen, with his communicative view of language, his work in foreign language teaching, *and* his pacifism, should have been attracted to the idea of an international language. And far from being an irrelevant parenthesis, his work, first on Ido, then on Novial, was an integral part of his linguistic production and ought to be analysed as such.

What we shall be concerned with here is Jespersen's place in the international language movement, the positions he took, and how they reflected his general ideas of language. The approach will be in accordance with Louis Hjelmslev's assessment in his obituary article on Jespersen, that this was

> an area where he could utilize both his theoretical views of grammar and his ideas of the greatest efficiency and the least effort, thus putting his theory at the service of practical life...

These efforts are not devoid of interest from a theoretical point of view, and ought not to be ignored by the theorists of language.

(Hjelmslev 1942-3:127)[2]

We shall, however, also have to consider the fact that, half a century later, a universally accepted auxiliary language remains a dream, and Jespersen's own child, Novial, little more than a footnote in histories of the international language movement.

1907: Choosing a language

Jespersen was catapulted into the centre of events in 1907 when the French philosopher Louis Couturat convened a meeting in Paris of representatives from a number of institutions and societies. In 1901 a 'Délégation pour l'adoption d'une langue auxiliaire internationale' had been set up, and now a committee under the auspices of the Delegation was to choose the best candidate for the role of international language. Jespersen became a vice president, along with Baudouin de Courtenay; the president was the German chemist Ostwald, later a Nobel Prize winner.

The main contenders were Esperanto and Idiom Neutral. Dr Zamenhof's Esperanto is of course still with us and will be dealt with below. It is characterized by a completely regular grammar, phonemic spelling, and a vocabulary that is to a large extent Romance but with an admixture of German and English. The number of words (roots) is kept to a minimum in favour of extensive use of affixes. Word-classes are signalled by invariable endings (-a for adjectives, -e for adverbs etc.).

In contrast, Idiom Neutral, the creation of W. Rozenberger and others at St Petersburg round the turn of the century, was based on the idea that an international language should build on what was already international, so the vocabulary was to utilize what was common to the major European languages, with no arbitrary morphological rules imposed. In practice, this pan-European project looked almost completely like a Romance language.

Idiom Neutral did not last long, but many later projects such as Occidental (1922) or present-day Interlingua, build on the same idea of seeking out the existing common elements (of a restricted number of languages) and placing less emphasis on regularity and building-blocks than Esperanto.

The important thing to note is that it was within this limited range, between the poles of regularity and naturalness, and especially over the principles of root selection and word formation, that the battle raged throughout Jespersen's lifetime.

There were some options that the Committee did not consider. We shall look briefly at those before continuing with the situation in 1907.

There are basically three possible approaches in the quest for a universal language: one is to select an existing national language; another is to construct a language in accordance with some a priori principles; a third is to construct a language that is based on certain existing languages.

One might perhaps have expected that Jespersen would have opted for the first solution. He had recently extolled the virtues of English in *Growth and Structure of the English Language* (1905), and he had more than 20 years behind him of theoretical and practical work in the area of English as a foreign language. But he had also stated the arguments against the adoption of English (or any other national language) as a world language. They were essentially these two (here quoted from *An International Language*):

1. a deliberate choice of any one language for such a purpose would meet with unsurmountable difficulties on account of international jealousies. (1928:18)

2. each of them is several times more difficult than a constructed language need be. (1928:21)

In this he was in line with the other members of the Committee. His attachment to English was, however, to play a decisive role later in the construction of Novial.

The second possibility, a language based on a priori principles, the Committee gave short shrift. This had been a preoccupation of the 17th and 18th centuries, when many projects had seen the light of day, some of them ingenious, many fanciful. The underlying idea was that it must be possible to express human knowledge in a logical manner rather than the illogical, unprincipled way in which the existing languages clouded thought. The idea, then, was to improve human language as such, to produce a perfect vehicle for thought, not just to create yet another imperfect language. The result was often a classificatory system of the thesaurus type rather than a workable means of communication.

When Jespersen got involved in the question of constructed languages, the spirit of the age had already swung firmly to the third possibility, the a posteriori solution: the future auxiliary language should be based on existing human languages. The distinction between a priori and a posteriori solutions is a handy one, but it may also exaggerate the new beginning. Despite the decision of the Committee not to consider a priori projects at all, rationalistic ideas were far from dead (and we shall see them advanced later by Edward Sapir). Most so-called a posteriori solutions have in fact strong elements of a priori thought in them, reminiscences of the quest for the ideal grammar and the ideal semantic structure. Even Jespersen, who was on the whole 'naturalistic', seized the opportunity to improve a little on human language in general, not just in the sense of making the auxiliary language simpler (that is inherent in all projects of this type) but also inventing certain rational solutions that had no foundation in the existing languages that formed the basis of Novial.

There was, then, at this 1907 gathering, a fundamental consensus that should not be obscured by the tale of dissension that we come to presently. A constructed language that displayed its a priori elements too openly did not stand a chance. Only 25 years earlier, Volapük had achieved considerable fame, now it was not even discussed.

Aidalivelös obis de bad

The accepted truth about Volapük today is that it was an unintelligible, unlearnable language. When reading A. L. Guérard's statement that Volapük was 'an object lesson which mankind did not forget' (1922:96), one is tempted to understand it in the negative sense that Volapük was a resounding failure. But he meant it in the positive sense that Volapük had demonstrated to the world that an articial language could work. It had been made public by its creator J. M. Schleyer, a German clergyman, in 1880, and within 10 years had established itself with clubs and congresses, textbooks and periodicals. Thousands of people had learned the language. Compared to earlier projects of the a priori type it was indeed easy and natural – it could be used and was used as a means of communication.

The success, however temporary, of Volapük shows that the time was ripe for the idea of a constructed language as such, but there must also have been some virtues to Volapük that distinguished it from earlier projects and pointed forward to a workable solution. Briefly, they were these: the orthography was strictly phonemic; the words (root forms) had a simple phonetic structure; the grammar was without exceptions, with fixed endings for number, case, word-class, etc. To take an example from the heading, *ob* means 'I', -i is the accusative marker (for nouns and pronouns alike), -s is plural, so *obi* is 'me', *obs* is 'we', and *obis* is 'us'.

Why did the Volapük movement collapse within a few years, to be superseded by Esperanto? Part of the explanation is possibly to be found in the a priori features of the language inherited from earlier projects, e.g. the classificatory system in parts of the vocabulary (all animal names ended in -af and so on) and an elaborate system of affixes to denote shades of meaning (-ös in the heading is an optative marker). But this in itself would hardly have condemned it; there are a priori features in other constructed languages.

Schleyer's German background was evident in the use of ä, ö, ü and in the declension of nouns in four cases, which may have dampened the enthusiasm of some, but also in the formation of compounds by juxtaposition of roots. This feature, combined with the complex system of affixation, led to long 'rebus words' which obscured the simple form of the roots. It was, in the words of Guérard, the synthetic method run riot.

Most detrimental to the sustained success of Volapük, however, were the unrecognizable roots. Even the intelligent reader may want to be informed at this stage that the heading actually means 'Deliver us from evil'. And that is an exceptionally easy example. Most of the vocabulary of Volapük was based on English, but *bad* is a rare case of unchanged borrowing; in most cases Schleyer changed the English word to conform with his principle of simple syllabic structure, so *world* became *vol* and *speak* became *pük* (the -a- in *Volapük* is a genitive marker).

Jespersen's points of criticism, as summed up later (1928:33-4), were these: the arbitrary grammatical system, the profusion of prefixes and suffixes, and the 'capricious distortions of the best-known words'. In other words, Volapük was unneccessarily difficult to learn. We shall return to the question of learnability at the end of the chapter, but for the moment only note that the fate of the Volapük movement had discredited any further projects along those lines. Jespersen, with the other members of the Committee, saw the solution elsewhere. Exactly where was a different matter.

Liberigu nin de la malbono
Liberigez ni del malajo

At the 1907 conference, Dr Zamenhof was represented by one of the leading French Esperantists, Louis de Beaufront, who ably laid out the case for Esperanto. It was a strong case. The grammar was simple, the vocabulary recognizable, and since publication in 1887 it had gained a considerable following. It worked.

Jespersen found much to admire in Zamenhof's product, but he had certain reservations. Some of these one may perhaps classify as minor irritants: the many sibilant sounds (no problem for Slavs), the use of circumflexed letters, the choice of -j as plural ending (from Greek). Some other characteristics of Esperanto were more profoundly in conflict with Jespersen's view of what an a posteriori language should be like:

Esperanto had an accusative case (the -n of *nin* above) and demanded concord between noun and adjective, with the result that you got strings like *belajn florojn* in the plural accusative. This was exactly the kind of redundancy that Jespersen had praised English for having got rid of.

Vowel endings were used in Esperanto to systematically denote word-class membership (the -a in the adjective *bela* and the -o in the noun *floro*). This a priori systematicity was most pronounced in the so-called Table of Correlative Words, a kind af grid where e.g. motive, time and possession were assigned the stems *ial, iam* and *ies* while e.g. interrogative and demonstrative were assigned the initial consonants k- and t-. The result, to give just two examples out of a total of 45, was *kial* = 'why' and *ties* = 'that person's'. Very ingenious, but not to the liking of someone who, like Jespersen, favoured a naturalistic solution, i.e. the utilization of as much as possible of what was common to the European languages.

Although the Table of Correlative Words was an extreme case, there was a similar conflict over the vocabulary in general. In the construction of any a posteriori language a balance has to be struck between root forms and derivational building-blocks. Zamenhof had deliberately sought to minimize the number of roots to be learned, and consequently relied extensively on a system of suffixes for language-internal word generation. Jespersen thought this was going too far, when e.g. 'mother' was *patrino* and 'to open' was *malfermi* (cf. the mal- of *malbono* in the heading above).

So, with all that there was to admire in Zamenhof's scheme, it could not be considered perfect, and Jespersen had in fact arrived at the

1907 conference in favour of choosing Idiom Neutral as the point of departure. But towards the end of the conference, the participants received an anonymous plan for a modified version of Esperanto which met some of the criticisms that Jespersen and others had levelled against it.

Nothing divides like a common cause, and the history of the promotion of an international language for mankind's peaceful cooperation is one of fierce feuds and personal bitterness. Jespersen saw himself in retrospect as a voice of reason, but he did become embroiled in some of the intense manoeuvring that goes under the name Ido Schism. 'Ido' was the pseudonym used by the author of the principles for a reform but stuck as the name of the resulting language, much as 'Esperanto' itself had started out as Zamenhof's pseudonym (='hoping person'). The id of 'Ido' was an Esperanto suffix meaning 'descendant of', and when following the ensuing intense fighting it is often hard to keep in mind that Ido was in fact just that: a proposal for a modification of Esperanto (compare the two versions in the heading of this section).

The idea now was that Jespersen and others, as a Permanent Commission – one step further removed from whatever authority the Delegation may have had – should work out the details for a reform of Esperanto and negotiate the suggestions with influential Esperantists.

They had clearly not taken the nature of the Esperanto movement into consideration. The response on the part of Zamenhof and the Esperantists' Lingva komitato was hostile. Jespersen bemoaned the conservatism and irrationality of the Esperantists, but in all fairness it should be observed that no movement will survive without a certain intransigence, and we shall have more to say later about Jespersen's apparent lack of understanding of what makes a movement successful.

Into this tense situation came Jespersen's discovery by accident of the identity of 'Ido'. The story is almost too good to be true: Jespersen received a letter from Couturat that had somehow got into the wrong envelope. It was intended for de Beaufront, and it seemed to imply that 'Ido' was none other than de Beaufront himself, the Esperanto champion! Jespersen was horrified and pressured de Beaufront to a public confession (quoted in Forster 1982:129).

To make the waters even muddier, we should add here that de Beaufront's confession probably was not quite the truth either! Andrew Large (1985:83) thinks it more likely that the author was Couturat; Forster (1982:143, note 66) suggests the possibility that de Beaufront formulated Couturat's ideas. In any case, peaceful cooperation on the project of reforming Esperanto was out of the question. Even today the mere mention of the names de Beaufront and Couturat will provoke furious reactions from Esperantists (Wood 1979:446).

In 1908 Zamenhof was in Copenhagen, and a meeting with Jespersen was arranged. It is in line with the preceding story that Jespersen was led up the back staircase of Zamenhof's hotel to avoid detection by other Esperantists. Zamenhof urged Jespersen to stop collaborating with the traitor de Beaufront.

> I answered that to me the question was in no way personal but scientific-practical, I would support the most perfect language, and I thought that Esperanto needed reforms. (1938: 133)

Jespersen momentarily lost some of his optimism, but he still considered the Ido proposals basically sound, and he took an active part in the working out of what had now become, rather than a plan for a reform of Esperanto, a competing language. He even became president of an Ido Academy, where Couturat as secretary took care of the organizational work. They had a quarrel over some practical matters, but Jespersen never officially resigned, and he continued to write for the Ido periodical *Progreso* until 1912.

1928: Constructing a language

Jespersen's reply to Zamenhof is symptomatic: an international language must be worked out on scientific principles; it cannot be a dogma. If Jespersen understood what it takes to make a movement a movement, he certainly did not want to have anything to do with what he considered the irrational sides of Esperantism.[3]

It must be the obvious goal of any constructor of an international auxiliary language to convince a large number of people that this language has a future, that it is worth investing effort in learning it. But Jespersen did not see any need for charismatic leaders, resistance to change, unflinching loyalty and devotion to the 'kara lingvo' which are probably some of the qualities that have kept the Esperanto movement together. It may not be the most perfect language devised, but in 1987, for the centennial celebration, 6,000 Esperantists gathered in Warsaw. The language is a living fact when so many other projects are forgotten.

Jespersen felt more at home with the Idists. He wanted, as he was later to formulate it, 'a language for the brain, not for the heart' (1928: 27), and the choice between various schemes should not depend exclusively on the public's whimsical preferences (1928:31). On what then?

In 1925 Jespersen met the wealthy American Mrs Alice Morris, a member of the Vanderbilt family, who had been instrumental in the foundation of an International Auxiliary Language Association as the forum for discussions about the principles for the construction of the ideal language.[4] Through her Jespersen met a number of congenial minds, among them Edgar de Wahl, the creator of Occidental, and the discussions of principles soon pushed him in the direction of practical application, working out a scheme of his own.

Jespersen's conclusion when he surveyed the wealth of proposed languages, the schisms and the constant bickerings, was not that of the Esperantists, that one existing system must be adhered to. He saw the lack of agreement as proof that all systems as yet devised had had obvious defects; 'the scientific and political world will not accept a language that can be justly and severely criticized by competent authorities' (1928:51). In other words, the debate would have to continue, but among men who were interested in a rational solution to a technical linguistic problem. He found that what had been criticized most in the various proposals was that the grammatical structure was unnecessarily complicated and that they deviated more than necessary from what was found in existing national languages.

Simple and natural, then, were to be the guiding words, and in *An International Language*, which we have already drawn on for the prehistory of Novial, Jespersen formulated these two principles:

> The less arbitrary and the more rational the forms, the more stable will they be –

and

> That international language is best which in every point offers the greatest facility to the greatest number. (1928:52)[5]

It is hard to overlook the inherent tension between the simple and rational on the one hand and the natural, pre-existing on the other. It is of course the opposition we noted earlier, and which can only be resolved through compromise solutions.

It is instructive to compare Jespersen at this point to Edward Sapir, whose article 'The Function of an International Auxiliary Language' appeared in 1931 together with Jespersen's 'Interlinguistics'.

Sapir rejected the thought of English as a world language because, contrary to the assumptions of many (English-speaking) people, English is not simple but 'a perfect hornet's nest of bizarre and arbitrary usages'. National languages are illogical –

> In fact, one may go so far as to say that it is precisely the apparent simplicity of structure which is suggested by the formal simplicity of many languages which is responsible for much slovenliness in thought, and even for the creation of imaginary problems in philosophy. (1931/1968:117)

It is clear that Sapir did not have only the practical aim – international communication – in mind, but continued the 18th century preoccupation with the creation of an ideal language as a vehicle for logical rigour.6 An international auxiliary language would have to be logically defensible at every point, so it is no wonder that Sapir found that no constructed language yet lived up to this exacting ideal.

In comparison, Jespersen's position was far from radical. Simplicity and regularity would have to be balanced with, and in many cases overridden by, what was common to the major European languages. Many perfectly logical constructions would have to be discarded on this account, and for a language that was to be an effective means of communication other considerations also would decide against logic, thus where Esperanto had *maldekstre* Jespersen chose *lefti* to avoid possible mishearings (1933/1960:678).

The vocabulary would be as far as possible common European. The constructors of Idiom Neutral had decided what was the most international word by counting occurrences in a number of European languages (most of them Romance, with inevitable consequences). Jespersen revised this procedure, in accordance with the dictum about the greatest facility for the greatest number, to a count not of languages but of the number of people who knew a certain word from their mothertongue (1928:163).

These were some of the principles underlying what Jespersen proudly announced as 'the first interlanguage ever framed by a professional philologist' (1928:59).

Nov international auxiliari lingue

> 'Ma lo ya have totim nulum sur se!' dikted un mikri infante.
> 'Men deo, audi li inosenten vose!' dikted li patro, e on murmurad a mutu tum kel li infante ha dikte.
> 'Lo have nulum sur se!' kriad finalim li toti popule.
> (1928:191)

We cannot go into the myriad of details that Jespersen had to busy himself with. A few examples will be selected to show some typical solutions.

First a minor but persistent problem in the area of pronunciation and spelling. We have already noted the profusion of sibilants and the use of circumflexed letters in Esperanto, which had s /s/, z /z/, ŝ /ʃ/, ĵ /ʒ/, c /ts/, ĉ /tʃ/ and ĝ /dʒ/. In other projects the letter c had been given different values, reflecting the different pronunciations that the letter has come to be used for in various European languages. Jespersen's solution was radical: he threw it out. The digraph ch appears, but only as a historically conditioned variant of sh, both to be pronounced either [ʃ] or [tʃ]. This feature of free variation he also adopted for [s] and [z], both written s (z went the way of c) and for j = [ʒ] or [dʒ]. In the specimen above, *vose* is either [-s-] or [-z-].

This reduction in the number of consonantal phonemes, together with the choice of a five-vowel system, limited Jespersen's possibilities for creating minimal pairs, but the limitation was offset by another break with the past. He gave up Esperanto's a priori feature of fixed vowel endings to mark word-classes, which had been taken over by Ido. Besides enabling him to introduce distinctions like *kasu* = 'example' vs *kase* = 'box', it left him free to use the three vowel endings -o/-a/-e for other purposes than as markers of nouns, adjectives and adverbs. Jespersen used them for two different purposes:

One was to denote sex, a use taken over from de Wahl's Occidental (1922), e.g. *filio* = 'son', *filia* = 'daughter', *filie* = 'son or daughter'. In the text above, *infante* appears in the sex-unspecified form while 'boy/girl' would be *infanto/infanta*. Other examples in the text are the male nouns *deo* and *patro* as well as the pronoun *lo* = 'he'. Unspecified for sex are *popule*, the nominal adjective *inosente*, and of course the non-animate *vose*. (We should note that Jespersen took the opportunity to solve a well-known problem of pronominal reference by his *le* = 'he or she' parallel with the unspecified plural *les* = 'they'.) The -o and -a forms were to be used for derivation where it was practical to indicate sex, but regularity was to be subordinate to the demand for a natural (i.e. common European) vocabulary, so 'mother' was not *patra* but *matra*.

113

The other use of these same endings was as derivational tools, thus the -o would turn a verb (e.g. *komensa* or *respekte*) into a noun denoting an act or a state (*komenso, respekto*). Nouns of the sex-unspecified type in -e could be turned into verbs, and we then got a threefold relationship: *danse* ('a dance') –> *dansa* ('to dance') –> *danso* ('dancing').[7]

Our final example of innovation will be the verbal system. Esperanto had a system with the vowels a/i/o as markers of present, past and future: *amas/amis/amos*, active participles *amanta/aminta/amonta*, passive participles *amata/amita/amota*. Jespersen found this 'totally artificial without any connexion with our natural linguistic habits' (1928: 108). What Jespersen felt to be the natural linguistic habit we can see in the specimen in the present tense *have*,[8] equal to the base form, and the past forms *dikted, murmurad* and *kriad*. The perfect *ha dikte* shows the preference for analytical expressions, other auxiliaries being *sal* and *ve* and for the passive *bli*. In fact Jespersen also allowed the past to be expressed as *did dikte* besides *dikted*. But he went one step further: the *dikte* of *ha dikte, bli dikte* etc. is the base form not an inflected participle. So there were points where Jespersen thought that even that advanced language English had not become natural enough.

Innovation and continuity

These three examples were meant to be representative of Jespersen's approach: his solution to problems that he saw in earlier systems, his ingenuity in the novel use of vowel endings, the way his preference for analytical expression and his general view of progress in language came out in his treatment of the verbal system.

Not all the solutions have been embraced by everybody. H. Jacob, who was on the whole favourably disposed, wondered whether the use of the e/a/o series for two different purposes did not make the practical application of the language more difficult (Jacob 1947:82). From G. Waringhien – who sees no viable alternative to Esperanto – we shall quote this scathing remark:

> Honestly, among all the projects presented after the appearance of Esperanto (I am talking here of projects that have been seriously devised and executed) can one find one that is less satisfactory, less harmonious and less practical?
>
> (Waringhien 1960:592)

What is of more concern to us here than the continued battle between Esperantists and the rest, is to repeat that Jespersen was working within a strictly circumscribed tradition. As Large sums it up: 'The main features of Novial differed in detail only from a number of earlier schemes' (1985:142). Jespersen's aim was to improve on earlier work on the creation of an a posteriori auxiliary language based on Western European languages. On many points he tried to strike a balance between the regularity of Esperanto/Ido and the 'naturalness' of Idiom Neutral and its descendant Occidental. Like Esperanto/Ido, Novial operated with a system of well-defined affixes, but they were not to be used for regular derivation if a common European root was available (as we saw 'mother' was *matra*, where Esperanto had *patrino*). He was prepared to go far in the direction of naturalness, in fact he subsequently reintroduced the much maligned letters c and z as a bow to tradition; *komensa* even became *comença* – a somewhat sad end to the old crusader against the circumflexed letters of Esperanto.

The naturalness criterion can be pretty subjective. To the German Schleyer it seemed perfectly natural to have the vowels ä, ö, ü and four cases; to the Pole Zamenhof a range of sibilants and an accusative to express e.g. direction were natural. Not so to Jespersen, but who else than a Dane would have found it imperative to do away with the distinction between voiced and unvoiced s? And there was a genitive in Novial (the -n of *inosenten*).

As to vocabulary, Jespersen's dictum about the greatest facility for the greatest number did not in fact produce a language that was markedly different in this respect from many earlier projects. Jespersen had

115

suggested that rather than counting languages, one should count the number of people who knew a certain form from their mother-tongue, but with the focus on Europe and the difficulty of finding many middle forms between English and German, the resulting vocabulary was in fact predominantly Romance. There was a certain Germanic admixture; the first page or so of the preface to *Novial lexike* yields the following: *dis (this), eme (aim), vud (would), strese (stress), tu (to); vorde (word* and German *Wort), mus (must* and German *muss); nur* (German *nur); bli* (Scandinavian *bli); vor (where* and German *wo* and Scandinavian *(h)vor).* All the rest is Romance.

Jespersen was quite conscious of this common European, and more specifically Romance, bias. As he wrote when he presented Novial:

> All recent attempts show an unmistakable family likeness, and may be termed dialects of one and the same type of international language. (1928:52)

He saw his own language as a contribution to further development and perfection, not as a radical new departure.

As we have seen, he took a couple of steps in the direction of English, and also introduced features that fitted in with his idea of progress in language even if they did not have a basis in English (the extended use of the base form of the verb, or the sex-unspecified pronouns), but he did not do everything that one might have expected.

In the preface to *Novial lexike* we find this characteristic statement:

> Progress in national languages has everywhere been in the direction of simple and analytical forms – this should be the guiding principle in the construction of an international language. (1930:19)

But although he did have a completely analytical verbal system, he also allowed a synthetic past. There was no accusative in Novial, but possession could be expressed both analytically and with a genitive suffix.

Some characteristics of English that Jespersen had often praised did not appear in Novial at all. There was little of the 'masculinity' of monosyllabic words ending in a consonant; Novial preserved the extensive use of vowel endings that most other projects had had. And because of the use of vowel endings to derive nouns from verbs and so on, we do not find the transfer of the unchanged stem form from one word-class to another, a feature of English which Jespersen had found so laudable.

Li emperen novi vestres?

We shall now step back from the details of the construction of auxiliary languages to ask a couple of general questions.

Ease of learning?

In the debate over the last 100 years, ease of learning has been a constantly advanced criterion. Arguments like the following crop up again and again: constructed languages are easier to learn than national languages; a constructed language must have a simple and regular grammar so that it is easy to learn; the root and affix forms of Volapük were unrecognizable, hence not easy to learn.

Easy for whom?

We have already touched on the Western European bias. This was openly admitted by Jespersen, perhaps sometimes with more complacency than we find tasteful today, but also with an open eye:

> it must be left to the future to work out the problem of a real world-language, if people are not content with a common European-American tongue. (1931/1960:729)

The future does not seem to have arrived yet – it is still not clear what the alternative could be. The completely neutral is the completely arbitrary, and few people, now as then, would like to consider the idea that Volapük was on the right track. Still, it should not be overlooked that Volapük was perhaps discredited less for a good reason (the synthetic method run riot) than for a bad reason: that it was not immediately palatable to educated Europeans.

Jespersen had another memento for the future: that we should learn from Chinese grammar and from Pidgins and Creoles (1931/1960:730). Again it is easy to point to Jespersen's actual European bias, less easy to claim that we are much wiser today.[9]

Within the European scene we have noted the Romance nature of the vocabulary of all the main contenders since Esperanto. The appearance of some German (*knabo* = 'boy') and English (*birdo*) in Esperanto seems to be mainly due to Zamenhof wanting to avoid a completely neo-Latin appearance (Guérard 1922:113). Jespersen's objective method of root-selection did not yield a drastically different result, and in any case – to quote Guérard –

> Granted that the method, properly applied, would make each separate word 'easiest for the greatest number of men', this would not be true of the language as a whole. (1922:245)

The incorporation of a few words from e.g. Russian will be no great assistance to Russians and a stumbling-block to many others. It will not make the auxiliary language truly international, any more than a couple of Japanese loans in Esperanto do (as proudly reported in Wood 1979: 442).

There is something even more unsettling in connection with the question of ease of learning, and it is one of the main points of Mario Pei's *One Language for the World* (1958): any language is easy if learned early. The whole argument about ease of learning hinges on one unstated assumption: that the international language must be learned by adults. It was immediately impressive when Jespersen gave a lecture in Ido at Copenhagen University and the audience, who had had little previous training in the language, understood everything (1938:135). It is less convincing as a demonstration of the superiority of Ido, or any other constructed language, when you consider that these unprepared listeners were people who had learned Latin, French, English and German.

It is certainly possible to maintain that the prime target group for an international auxiliary language is adults, or adults of the educated class, or, as Alexander Gode, one of the constructors of the neo-Latin Interlingua, has argued, that scientists all over the world must learn the essential western scientific vocabulary anyway (Pei 1958:171). But the question of ease of learning does recede into the background if we accept Pei's idea that a truly international language must be a second language learned by all when they are still children.

A constructed language?

In fact the very distinction between national and constructed languages becomes less important in this light – except for one area where you *can* talk about intrinsic ease and intrinsic difficulty: orthography (Pei 1958: 187).

There remains the argument about the 'unsurmountable difficulties on account of international jealousies' if a national language is chosen for the role of universal auxiliary language. This argument, which has been put forward by all adherents of constructed languages, is indeed a formidable one. But it is a political not a linguistic argument, and may not be permanently true of all national languages. In our time we may have to rule out English and Russian as the universally accepted language, but it is not at all clear why a neo-Latin constructed language should stand a better chance of acceptance than Spanish.

Neither stands a good chance anyway. As J. R. Firth wrily commented in 1937, 'world languages are made not by amateur grammarians but by world powers' (1964:70). And we could add: not by professional grammarians either. It is not logic and ease that have given English its prominent position in the world today.

119

A *testing-ground*

The purpose of the preceding sections was to re-examine some common assumptions among constructors of auxiliary languages. It was in no way intended to detract from their merits; the linguistic ingenuity remains. But rather than judge the projects by their actual or potential contribution to international communication, we are better advised to consider the construction of international auxiliary languages as a testing-ground for linguistic thought: what language is and what it can be, how much can be regular and how much must be arbitrary, even what is good and bad in a language. In Jespersen's case, to see his life-long preoccupation with auxiliary languages and his creation of Novial not as a heroic failure but as a revealing application of his linguistic thought.

Notes

1. In the rest of the chapter we shall avoid the labels 'artificial' and 'natural' and use 'constructed' and 'national' instead. Jespersen made the point about the artificial features of natural languages and the natural features of artificial languages in e.g. 'Nature and Art in Language' (1929).
2. Quotations in French and Danish have been tacitly translated.
3. There is much about this in Forster (1982), including a sociological survey of British Esperantists.
4. It was the IALA that eventually produced the neo-Latin Interlingua, in 1952.
5. The latter variation on a theme by Bentham he had first formulated in 1908, i.e. in the wake of the Paris conference.
6. There was also a link with a contemporary trend among philosophers of language.
7. Jespersen later gave up the -o derivation in this case, using instead the verbal base form in -a as a verbal noun.

8. *Have/haved* = 'possess/-ed' was distinct from the auxiliary *ha/had*.
9. Pei (1958:157) mentions an attempt (presumably abortive) from the 1950s to combine English one-syllable roots with a Chinese-type syntax.

Bibliography

Firth, J.R. 1964. ' "Real characters and universal languages". Debabeliz-ation', Ch. 6 of *The Tongues of Men*. London: Watts & Co, 1937; also in *The Tongues of Men and Speech*. Oxford University Press.

Forster, P.G. 1982. *The Esperanto Movement*. The Hague: Mouton.

Guérard, A.L. 1922. *A Short History of the International Language Movement*, London: Unwin; reprint Westport: Hyperion Press, 1979.

Hjelmslev, L. 1942-3. 'Nécrologie: Otto Jespersen'. *Acta Linguistica* 3/1 119-30.

Jacob, H. 1943. *Otto Jespersen: His Work for an International Auxiliary Language*. Loughton, International Language (Ido) Society of Great Britain.

Jacob, H. 1947. *A Planned Auxiliary Language*.London: Dennis Dobson Limited.

Jespersen, O. 1921. 'Artificial Languages after the World War'. In: *Two Papers on International Language in English and Ido*; English version in *Selected Writings* 707-14.

Jespersen, O. 1921. 'History of Our Language'. In: *Two Papers on International Language in English and Ido*; English version in *Selected Writings* 698-706.

Jespersen, O. 1928. *An International Language*. London: George Allen & Unwin; Introduction in *Selected Writings* 680-97.

Jespersen, O. 1929. 'Nature and Art in Language'. *American Speech* 5; in *Linguistica: Selected Papers in English, French and German* (1933) 434-53; also in *Selected Writings* 660-79.

Jespersen, O. 1930. *Novial lexike. International Dictionary, Diction-naire international, Internationales Wörterbuch.* London: George Allen & Unwin. Preface in *Selected Writings* 715-19.

Jespersen, O. 1931. 'Interlinguistics'. In: *International Communication: A Symposium on the Language Problem* by Herbert N. Shenton et al. London: Kegan Paul 95-120; also in *Selected Writings* 720-31.

Jespersen, O. 1938. *En sprogmands levned.* Copenhagen: Gyldendal.

Jespersen, O. 1960. *Selected Writings of Otto Jespersen.* London: George Allen & Unwin.

Large, A. 1985. *The Artificial Language Movement.* London: Basil Blackwell.

Sapir, E. 1931. 'The Function of an International Auxiliary Language'. In: Shenton, H.N. et al., *International Communication: A Symposium on the Language Problem* 65-94; also in *Selected Writings of Edward Sapir in Language, Culture and Personality*, ed. D.G. Mandelbaum, Berkeley and Los Angeles: University of California Press (1968) 110-21.

Waringhien, G. 1960. 'Le problème d'une langue auxiliaire mondiale'. *Norsk tidsskrift for sprogvidenskap* 19, 591-4.

Wood, R.E. 1979. 'A Voluntary Non-Ethnic, Non-Territorial Speech Community'. In: *Sociolinguistic Studies in Language Contact: Methods and Cases*, ed. W.F. Mackey & J. Ornstein. The Hague, Paris, New York: Mouton 433-50.

Acknowledgement: I want to thank Paul Christophersen and Mike Davenport for comments on an earlier version.

Hans Vejleskov

OTTO JESPERSEN'S THINKING ABOUT CHILD LANGUAGE

Introduction

In this article I shall attempt to present a picture of Otto Jespersen as a language psychologist by reviewing his observations and ideas on young children's verbal expressions, on their acquisition of their mother tongue, and on the relationship between language and thought.

Although Jespersen was known, above all, as an outstanding linguist, he wrote several books on themes belonging to the field of language psychology,[1] and it may be interesting to consider these from the standpoint of modern psycholinguistics and psychology of language.[2] Taking into account the attention paid to literacy within this field during the last few years, I shall also discuss Jespersen's views on writing versus speech. Finally, in the spirit of Jespersen himself, I shall add some remarks on educational consequences.

Although it is always difficult – indeed impossible – to distinguish sharply between description and explanation, and although explanations in the field of language development often involve ideas about the relationship between language and thought, each of the following Sections 1-3 will deal – primarily – with one of these topics.

1. Characteristics of children's talk

In his most extensive description of child language, *Nutidssprog* ... (1916) or *Börnesprog* (1923) (cf. Note 1), Jespersen emphasizes that he is studying this topic as a linguist. By this statement he explicitly dissociates himself from the contemporary works of psychologists and educationalists such as W. Wundt, W. Stern and Vilhelm Rasmussen.[3]

Most scholars of today would maintain that collaboration between linguists and psychologists is needed for this 'psycholinguistic' enterprise. In addition, it is natural to assume that every linguist must hold a psychological theory, and correspondingly that every psychologist studying child language must have a theory of language. Certainly, Jespersen expressed many views on psychological matters such as learning, thinking, awareness, child development, etc. His criticism of the psychologists of that time concerned not only their inadequate knowledge about language: he attacked them on their own ground. Three examples of such criticism will be mentioned here:

(1) Jespersen states that, as he himself adopts a purely linguistic approach, he does not expect to draw such excessive and high-flown conclusions as those drawn by scholars who seek – through the study of children's language – to learn about sublime matters such as the development of children's minds, the birth of self-awareness, or the development of mankind.[4]

(2) He criticizes the statement of the founder of the first psychological laboratory, W. Wundt, that the language of children is generated by their environment, the children themselves taking part in the process only in a very passive way (a view shared by many present-day psychologists). According to Jespersen, this is one of the most incorrect statements ever written by an outstanding scientist.[5]

(3) Mentioning the various countings of children's vocabulary at different ages, Jespersen says that the observers often do not realize the difficulties involved. For instance, they do not make it clear whether the words counted are those that the child has understood or those that he has actually used. Nor do they state exactly what is to be counted as a word: are 'I', 'me', 'we', and 'us' one, two or four words? Is 'teacup' a new word for a child who already knows 'tea' and 'cup'? In this connection, Jespersen recommends us to in-

vestigate what words children do *not* know. Such studies will lead to a better insight into the development of vocabulary and word meanings, he argues.[6]

The first two points are concerned with theoretical problems to which we shall return in Section 2, but the third deals with the observation and description of child language. It constitutes a very lucid example of Jespersen's ideas, for it makes clear that he himself adopts a purely linguistic approach to child language.

In his description of children's language, Jespersen introduces three stages: (i) the stage of *screaming*, (ii) the stage of *babbling*, and (iii) the stage of *talking*, which is further divided into the period of *own language* and the period of *common language*. The development during the last stage is described in four separate sections dealing with sounds, words, forms and sentences respectively. In contrast to modern psycholinguistics, grammar is treated rather briefly in the last two sections, whereas word meaning, word formation, etc., are dealt with in larger sections.[7] This fact is naturally reflected in the following comments.

Sounds

On the subject of *sounds* Jespersen makes the interesting comment that even if the scream is not a message on the part of the baby himself, it is regarded as a message by the parents, 'and so the path towards something like language is entered'.[8] This accords with the fact that during the last decade child psychology has studied early mother-infant communication and underlined the importance of behavioural synchronization as well as the mother's search for meaning in the child's behaviour.

With respect to sound development, Jespersen does not rely upon 'the law of least effort' put forward by Schultze. However, he states that among the consonants, the labials, *p, b* and *m* are the earliest sounds, probably because the child can see the movements of his mother's lips.[9] During the stage of babbling (with its characteristic syllable series such as *da-da-da* ... or *ne-ne-ne* ...) many sounds or sound combinations are pronounced correctly by the child, although at a later stage he does not master them. Jespersen explains this fact in terms of the difference between, on the one hand, involuntary and effortless action and, on the other, voluntary, planned action, a difference that modern cognitive psychology often notices.

During the last part of this stage, the child shows 'the first understanding': he discovers that certain words or phrases said by other persons *mean* something.

> When my son was one year old, the nurse taught him the pat-a-cake play. Whenever these words were said, he began clapping his hands ... Even when the words were used as part of a fairly long sentence, they had the same effect.

> The understanding of speech is always earlier than the ability to say the same oneself – often much earlier. This fact is shown especially by the direction of the child's eyes ...[10]

However, Jespersen warns us against relying upon that kind of observation:

> In fact it is not until the child speaks himself that we can know for certain what he really understands, and even then it may sometimes be difficult to plumb the depths of a child's understanding.[11]

When we consider the period of own language, we are dealing with *language proper*, i.e., sounds connected with thoughts.[12] Although Jespersen presents many interesting observations concerning *sounds* in this period and, especially, in the period of common language, we shall now proceed to the development of words in children, which was the subject of the most extensive observation on Jespersen's part.

Words

The move from the study of sounds to the study of words means a transition from the external to the internal aspect of language, for now we have to deal with the complex patterns of concepts or categories 'in the world of sensations and thought encountering the child',[13] and during the period of own language we observe special words differing not only in sound combinations but also diverging in meaning and categorization.

> A little girl of two called a horse *he* (Danish *hest*), and divided the animal kingdom into two groups, (1) horses, including all four-footed things, even a tortoise, and (2) fishes (pronounced *iz*) including all that moved without use of feet, for example birds and flies ... A boy who had a pig drawn for him, the pig being called *öf*, at the age of 1;6 used *öf* (1) for a pig, (2) for drawing a pig, (3) for writing in general.[14]

However, Jespersen warns us not to draw conclusions about word meanings from observations of this kind, as young children may well not designate things in the way grown-up persons do at all. Perhaps children only express the perception of certain connections or coincidences, he argues, and he adds some examples of 'misunderstandings' by children due to lack of precision or the use of childish words by an adult.

Moving to the period of common language, Jespersen deals with the following phenomena:

(a)   The words *father* and *mother*.
(b)   'Abstract' and ambiguous words such as *king* or *heaven* and *son/sun* or *child*.
(c)   Metaphors and intensifying additions such as *stone-dead* or *ice-cold* (a young boy once said: 'It is ice-warm').
(d)   Examples of children learning the derivative meaning earlier than the original meaning of a word.

(e)   The increase of children's vocabulary.

(f)   Words that are difficult because of

      (1)   their outer form, i.e. they are identical in sound with another word;

      (2)   their difficult (abstract) meaning.

(g)   Children's awareness of language.

(h)   Numerals.

(i)   Other 'shifters' (than *father* and *mother*) such as *the one* and *the other*, or *I, me, you*, etc. [15]

In addition to issues (b), (c) and (f) in a later chapter Jespersen presents his well-known interesting and amusing examples of *humour*, i.e., examples of children's funny misunderstandings of words or phrases, especially from stanzas of hymns or biblical history.[16] Although, unfortunately, these Danish examples cannot be translated into English, it must be mentioned here that they serve not only as examples of children's naive or superficial cognition: in line with the other groups of observations they appear as factual descriptions from which something about child language can be learnt. *Educationally* we can learn to express ourselves carefully and to avoid overestimating children's ability to understand. More importantly, we are taught a *psychological* lesson from these striking examples, namely that a child's acquisition of his mother tongue is, *in general*, a complex process of guessing, supposing and inventing, not only in the field of language but also in the fields of reality and conception.

Forms

With respect to *form*, Jespersen claims that the acquisition of grammar is not due to an instinct:

        ... when people ... say that it all 'comes quite of itself,' I must strongly demur: so far is it from 'coming of itself' that it demands extraordinary labour on the child's part.[17]

He further explains that even if many forms are to be ascribed to imitation and analogy, we must also face the fact that 'without being conscious of it, each of us ... now and then really creates something never heard before by us or anybody else'.[18]

In addition to the description of the gradual emergence of the forms of nouns, adjectives and verbs,[19] Jespersen also regards word-formation as an example of children's creative thinking.

> A child who does not know the word 'spade' may call the tool a *digger*; he may speak of a lamp as a *shine*. He may say *it suns* when the sun is shining (cf. it rains), or ask his mother to *sauce* the pudding. It is quite natural that the enormous number of nouns and verbs of exactly the same form in English (*blossom, care, drink, end, ...* etc.) should induce children to make new verbs according to the same pattern. I quote a few examples given by O'Shea: 'I am going to *basket* the apples' ... 'I needled him' (put a needle through a fly) ... Sometimes a child will make up a new word through 'blending' two, as when Hilary M. (1;8 to 2;0) spoke of *rubbish* = the *rub*ber to pol*ish* the boots. Beth M. (2;0) used *breakolate* from *break*fast and choc*olate*.[20]

Jespersen's emphasis on the way that children are active and creative in learning their mother tongue should undoubtedly be seen in the light of his interest in the history of language, to which he assumes that children have contributed in several respects.[21]

Finally, let me bring out another point made by Jespersen in this connection. We are, he says,

> so accustomed to see sentences in writing with a little space left after each word, that we have got altogether wrong

conceptions of language as it is spoken. Here words follow one another without the least pause till the speaker hesitates for a word ... 'Not at all' sounds like 'not a tall'.22 It therefore requires ... a great deal of ... analysis on the part of the child to find out what is one and what two or three words ... A girl (2;6) used the term *Tanobijeu* whenever she wished her younger brother to get out of her way. Her parents finally discovered that she had ... shortened [the] phrase ... 'Tend to your own business' ... A child who had been praised with the words, 'You are a good boy,' said to his mother, 'You are a good boy, mother' ... [And] children will often say *napple* for 'apple' through a misdivision of 'an-apple'.23

Sentences

With respect to *sentences*, Jespersen at first explains that

in the first period the child knows nothing of grammar ... 'Up' means 'I want to get up' or 'Lift me up'; 'Hat' means 'put on my hat,' or ... 'I have my hat on,' or 'Mamma has a new hat on' ... But when we say that such a word means what we should express by a whole sentence, this does not amount to saying that the child's 'Up' *is* a sentence, or a sentence-word, as many of those who have written about these questions have said. We might just as well assert that clapping our hands is a sentence ... expressing 'It is splendid' (!).24

Later he stresses the importance of *echoism*,25 and proceeds to the phenomena of

– negations
– questions, and
– prepositions.

130

> Stern makes the interesting remark that when the tendency to use prepositions first appears, it grows far more rapidly than the power to discriminate one preposition from another; with his own children there came a time when they employed the same word as a sort of universal preposition ... Hilda used *von*, Eva *auf*. I have never observed anything corresponding to this among Danish children ...
>
> The first use of prepositions is always in set phrases learnt as wholes, like 'go to school', 'go to pieces', 'lie in bed', 'at dinner'. Not till later comes the power of using prepositions in free combinations, and it is then that mistakes appear ... A little girl was in her bath, and hearing her mother say: 'I will wash you in a moment', answered: 'No you must wash me in the bath' ...[26]

This Section may well be concluded with Jespersen's observation that the study of children's utterances illuminates the fact that 'learning a language implies among other things learning what you may *not* say in that language, even though no reasonable ground can be given for the prohibition'.[27]

2. Reflections on language development

It will be recalled from Section I that Jespersen repeatedly mentions that language development is a matter of activity on the part of the child: 'the little brain' is continuously attentive and creative. But what kind of learning process is going on? This question, which is a very natural one from the point of view of modern psycholinguistics, is briefly dealt with by Jespersen. He states – like Noam Chomsky – that imitation (and other simple processes of learning?) cannot fully account for children's acquisition of language, since a certain amount of creativity and consciousness must be assumed, but he does not specify the process itself.

However, two questions which are discussed by Jespersen and which also represent fundamental approaches in modern psychology of language, may throw some light upon this problem.

The basic nature of language

The first question is that of the basic nature of language, i.e., whether language development must be understood *primarily* in terms of the performing of *speech acts*, or in terms of *cognition and information*.

Broadly speaking, language psychology has traditionally focussed upon cognition and information. Thus the crux of the matter was thought to be that the child, like Helen Keller, discovered that everything has a name. Words or phrases were signs representing things, qualities or events, so that through language, the child could (a) deal with non-present phenomena, and (b) transmit his observations and thoughts to other people. However, during the last few decades there has been an increasing interest in 'pragmatics' among linguists, psychologists and philosophers.[28] Still speaking in rather general terms, it seems important, in the psychology of language, to distinguish between two approaches to 'language function':

(1) The approach of conversational techniques, i.e., the study of turn-taking, intonation, etc.
(2) The approach of speech act theory, i.e., the study of the functions of utterances (or intentions on the part of the speaker) including the ability to utilize the unspoken, implicit elements of the context.

Both of these phenomena seem to be included in the concept of 'communicative competence', which is often, however, defined rather opaquely.

As mentioned above, Jespersen observed that the infant's scream is regarded as a message by the parents. Elsewhere he elaborates on his observations:

Many investigators have asserted that the child's first utterances are not means of imparting information, but always an expression of the child's wishes and requirements. This is certainly somewhat of an exaggeration, since the child quite clearly can make known its joy at seeing a hat or a plaything ... but the statement still contains a great deal of truth, for without strong feelings a child would not say much, and it is a great stimulus to talk that he very soon discovers that he gets his wishes fulfilled more easily when he makes them known by means of certain sounds.[29]

In his discussion[30] of the young child's surprisingly rapid learning of his mother tongue, even though he has no experience, even though his 'teachers' are untrained and unsystematic, and even though he receives only oral instruction, Jespersen criticizes several traditional explanations.[31] His own answer 'lies partly in the child itself, partly in the behaviour towards it of the people around it'.[32] He stresses that in the first years of life the child is more intelligent than later in the sense that during this period he is best capable of grasping new things and adapting to them; furthermore, his mother is talking to him all day,[33] in all possible situations, and in such a way that various non-verbal expressions supplement speech – and last but not least, in such a way that the relation between mother and child is very warm and personal, because she is not primarily a teacher.

Thus Jespersen is not in agreement with the Chomskyan theory of inborn structures and dispositions to learn the rules of transformation. Rather he is, to a certain extent, in line with modern ideas about the functional or pragmatic basis of *early* language development. However, when he discusses development in the period of common language, he makes no comments whatsoever on speech acts or communicative competence in a broader sense. Accordingly, in his review of F. de Saussure's *Cours de Linguistique...*(1916), Jespersen does not appreciate the distinction between *langue* and *parole*.

In his review of R.L. Garner's *The Speech of Monkeys* (1893), he accepts the idea that monkeys do have a language, because a small number of words, each of which refers to a certain class of things or a certain kind of emotional state, had been identified by Garner. According to Jespersen, these words are clearly addressed to another individual who is expected to respond, although monkeys do not carry on continuous conversations. This is interesting, because recent research seems to conclude that apes have no verbal language, but that they are able to learn to communicate by means of a simple sign language. More importantly, it is interesting because it shows that Jespersen could not transcend the notion that 'language proper' is mainly a matter of sounds connected with thoughts (cf. p. 126 above), although he made brilliant psychological observations of verbal interaction, and clearly understood the importance of the communicative context.

Linguistic awareness

During the last 4-8 years, language psychologists have paid much attention to *linguistic awareness*. For example the Swedish psychologist I. Lundberg has become quite well known for his efforts to promote linguistic awareness in pre-school children, based upon the assumption that a certain degree of linguistic awareness will benefit their learning to read and write.[34]

In this connection it is interesting to note that Jespersen consistently discusses to what extent the young child is aware of the phonetic, semantic and grammatical phenomena he is about to master.[35] With regard to sounds, he correctly remarks that the growing awareness of pronunciation may imply a temporary uncertainty corresponding to the uncertainty shown by adults when suddenly reflecting on the way they move their legs. He also points out that sometimes children are aware of errors by other speakers, although they make the same errors themselves, and adds that

> it is certain that ... the little brain is working and even consciously working, though at first [the child] has not sufficient command of speech to say anything about it.[36]

Moreover, he presents some good observations of children hesitating or whispering when they are about to say a word that they know is a difficult one (cf. Note 22).

With respect to grammar, Jespersen directly asks whether 'the little brain' *thinks* about the different forms and their use.[37] His own answer is that although young children do not think in the same way as in formal grammar teaching, many observations suggest that some thinking is going on: 'Papa, hast du mir was mitgebringt/gebrungen/gebracht?' asked a German child of two years, and occasionally other young children have directly expressed their insight into some grammatical rule, e.g., the inflection of a strong verb. He adds that we have to rely on such spontaneous expressions since it would be idle to ask children if and what they think about these things.

Finally Jespersen mentions children's play with language:

> It is also amusing to alter proper words consciously. Thus Frans (2;6) amused himself by making his vowels deep and round ... [And] many children early show an inclination to rhyme and combine words rhythmically.[38]

In conclusion, it may be stated that modern psychologists can learn much from Jespersen about how to observe child language in a way that combines openness and critical sense. Furthermore, Jespersen realizes how significant it is that children understand that the utterances of other people *mean* something, and that their own utterances must be experienced as having *an effect*. However, the activity and creativity of 'the little brain' concern mainly the struggle to grasp the semantic and grammatical 'unsystematic regularities' of the mother tongue.

3. Language and thought

The conclusion of Section 2 makes it evident that Jespersen has considered the classic problem of the relationship between language and thought, which unfortunately has become a rather confused problem because of the different meanings attributed to 'language' as well as 'thought'. Among other things, the relationship between language and thought may thus refer to the following, clearly different, questions:

A. Do children reflect on linguistic and/or communicative phenomena?
B. Does the way children talk, e.g., their word meanings or their grammar, reflect their conceptions of and reasoning about various extralinguistic phenomena?
C. Are children's propositions and explanations a direct path to discovering their perception and understanding?
D. Is a certain degree of mastery of the vocabulary and structure of the mother tongue a necessary condition for the attainment of a certain intellectual level?
E. Does the mastery of certain uses of language, i.e., certain utterance functions or speech acts, constitute such a condition?
F. Is a certain intellectual development a prerequisite for the acquisition of one or the other aspect of language (*langue/parole*)?

Whereas question A was considered in Section 2, and questions D-F were not discussed by Jespersen, the two questions about children's thinking being reflected by their language are given some consideration. However, to Jespersen questions B-C became narrower:

B'. Do children's *word meanings* reflect their *concept formation*?
C'. Are children's propositions and explanations – and *questions* – especially with respect to *vocabulary*, a direct path to discovering their *concepts*?

136

Thus, in an article written in 1916, Jespersen discusses children's concept formations with particular reference to issues (a), (b), (f) and (i) enumerated on p. 127-8 above.[39] His point of departure is the question of the emergence of *universals* or *general concepts* in children.

> What Stern tells about his own boy is certainly exceptional, perhaps unique. The boy ran to a door and said *das*?, his way of asking the name of a thing. They told him 'Tür'. He then went to two other doors in the room, and each time the performance was repeated. He then did the same with the seven chairs in the room. Stern says, 'As he thus makes sure that the objects that are alike ... have also the same name, he is on his way to general conceptions'. We should, however, be wary of attributing general ideas to little children.[40]

Jespersen adds that to children nouns are generally proper names and points to the words *father* and *mother* as particularly clear examples.

In view of the fact that Jespersen himself deals with *metaphors* (as words or phrases that are difficult for the child to *understand*), it is natural here to mention a modern theory stating that to the young child *each word* has the character of a metaphor: it is always heard and understood for the first time in one concrete context (e.g., 'open the door'), and so in the next context (e.g., 'open your mouth') it will necessarily appear in a figurative sense.[41]

Jespersen's discussion of the problem of words and concepts is mainly in terms of the obvious difficulties that kinship relations present to children. In this connection it might be interesting to note that about twenty-five years later Jean Piaget introduced his famous conception of 'concrete operations', which are the regulators of acting and thinking in children aged 7-13, and which are described by means of a certain set of 'logical groupings'. But with special reference to the operations of kinship relations, he additionally assumed the existence of a set of 'infra-logical groupings'.[42]

Finally, Jespersen presents a number of examples of words that are difficult for various reasons (cf. p. 128 above), some of which are ... 'used incorrectly by children because their concept delimitations differ from those of adults'.

Thus Jespersen mainly considers question B' (p. 136 above) and apparently holds that word meanings do reflect the concepts formed by children. However, he also expresses the view (in particular emphasized by Soviet psychology) that through the use of language the child acquires the conceptual frameworks of society:

> ... gradually a high degree of accuracy is obtained, the fittest meanings surviving – that is ... those that agree best with those of the surrounding society. And thus the individual is merged in the society, and the social character of language asserts itself through the elimination of everything that is the exclusive property of one person only.[43]

4. Speech and writing

Sections 1-3 solely take oral language into account, though with the added observation by Jespersen that only the acquisition of written language makes it clear to the child how oral utterances are divided into words (p. 130 above). His article about cursing and swearing (1911) presents another example of the importance of written language for our analysis of speech: the original meaning as well as the self-contradictory character of a number of oaths could hardly be seen without studying them in written form.

This shows that question C' (p. 136 above) can be answered in the affirmative: the mastery of *written* language influences the conception of linguistic phenomena. However, it is important to note that all the questions A-F can be asked in such a way that they particularly deal with the relationship between *written* language and thought. This is a very fundamental exercise within the modern study of *literacy*, which attempts to explore what it means for a person to be able to read and write.[44] Thus this research discipline runs counter to the traditional psychology of reading and writing, which rather one-sidedly studies the conditions governing the learning of these language skills.

Jespersen for his part chooses a third approach as he considers three methodological means of facilitating the elementary learning of reading and writing:[45]

(1)   The traditional arbitrary names of the letters must be replaced by their most common sound representations.

(2)   One must never carve up words of two or more syllables by means of hyphens.

(3)   During the first period of instruction all words must be written in phonetic script regardless of the correct spelling.

These rather extreme recommendations have never been followed in Danish schools, but the phonetic method of teaching reading has – in a modified form – had a significant influence. However, Jespersen's very approach shows that to him written language is derived from speech, and does not constitute a special 'secondary' language having a certain influence upon the learner's conception and reasoning.

Finally it must be remarked that the effect that the written language has upon the awareness and conception of language is, as Jespersen mentions, highly relevant to the field of foreign-language learning. The ease with which a 3-5-year-old child learns a second language, compared with the difficulties shown by 12-13-year-old children in school, can partly be explained by the fact that the latter cannot help analyzing the foreign language in terms of their reflective knowledge about the mother tongue.[46]

Now the problems of foreign-language learning will not be discussed here. It therefore only remains for me to mention that in his discussion of bilingualism among pre-school children,[47] Jespersen says that the advantage of an early mastery of two languages may well be bought too dearly, because some observations suggest that bilingual young children learn neither of the languages perfectly. He does not mention the question of whether such children are inclined to think more about language and thus become more motivated and – perhaps – better prepared for the acquisition of written language.

5. Educational consequences

These final reflections on Jespersen's thinking about child language are not concerned with school-teaching. However, as *linguistic* thinking about young children's language necessarily involves some psychological ideas (cf. p. 124 above), so psychological and linguistic observations of language development in young children are of course followed by reflections on *educational* matters. In fact, Sections 1-4 already contain such reflections.

Above all, it must be said that although much research has been done in the field of child language during the last 70 years, no advice of any importance can be added to that given by Jespersen about parents' behaviour towards their young children. Two years ago when I wrote a short elementary book on child language for parents and pre-school teachers,[48] I included many examples from Jespersen's works, not only because they are relevant and often amusing, but also because they are written in a positive and warm spirit. Ordinary parents do not need to be told about all the possible dangers that might follow from neglecting their children's language. Rather they need to be inspired to enjoy their children's conversation so that they will be encouraged to talk with them. Jespersen himself says:

> The most important rule (for parents) is to give the child plenty of opportunity to hear the language in its purest and best form, and to see to it that the child meets friendly children and grown-ups who will follow his progress with sympathy.[49]

In subsequent pages he adds a few direct instructions:

(1) Parents should not correct children's errors too often and too emphatically.
(2) Parents should not speak in a childish way themselves, in pronunciation or sentence length or form.

Finally, he discusses the question of getting children to learn poems by heart. Although he himself demonstrated how children often misunderstand hymns (cf. p. 128 above), this must not, he says, be taken to mean that parents should not read poems to their children: misunderstandings and phrases that are not fully grasped do not harm children, who often love poems, rhymes, and jingles. And Jespersen adds that too much understanding may be a bad thing:

> To me, there is no doubt about it that the disinclination of many young people to read good books is ... [partly] due to the fact that as schoolchildren they were made to go through some of the greatest works in their language in a most laborious way.[50]

By these considerations Jespersen indirectly states that parents' reading aloud to their children is an important part of the activities that further the development of language. He also rightly emphasizes that the activities of guessing, analyzing and inventing that 'the little brain' engages in are by no means solely an intellectual matter. They contain elements of play, amusement, aesthetics, wonder and mystery as well.

Hans Vejleskov

Notes

1. The following works by Jespersen form the background of this article:

Books:
Studier over engelske kasus. Copenhagen: Klein, 1891. (*Progress in Language*, London: Swan Sonnenschein, 1894.)
How to Teach a Foreign Language, London: Allen & Unwin, 1904. (12th impression 1961. Danish original: *Sprogundervisning*, Copenhagen: Gyldendal, 1901, 2nd ed. (revised) 1933.)
Nutidssprog hos Børn og Voksne, ('Today's Language in Children and Adults'), Copenhagen: Gyldendal, 1916. (2nd ed.: *Børnesprog* ('Child Language'), Copenhagen: Gyldendal, 1923.)
Language, Its Nature, Development and Origin, London: Allen & Unwin, 1922. (Part II, on child language, is a short version of *Nutidssprog*, etc., 1916.)
Sproget: Barnet, Kvinden, Slægten, ('Language: Children, Women, Generations'), Copenhagen: Gyldendal, 1941.
Efficiency in Linguistic Change, Copenhagen: Munksgaard, 1941.

Articles:
'Den nye Sprogundervisnings Program'. *Vor Ungdom*, 1886, pp. 353-81. (About the new method in foreign language teaching.)
'Abernes Sprog'. *Tilskueren*, April 1893, pp. 304-17. (About a book by R.L. Garner on the language of apes.)
'Om banden og sværgen'. In: *Festskrift til H.F. Feilberg*, Copenhagen, 1911, pp. 33-40. (About cursing and swearing.)
'Børns Begrebsdannelse'. *Tilskueren*, Feb. 1916. (On concept formation in children.)
Review of F. de Saussure, *Cours de Linguistique Générale. Nordisk Tidsskrift for Filologi*, 4th series, *vol. 6*, 1917, pp. 37-41. A French translation of this review is found in *Linguistica* (Co-

penhagen: Munksgaard, 1933), pp. 109-15.
Interview with Jespersen about child language. Broadcast by Danmarks Radio, 1941.

2. The term 'psychology of language' is used here to denote a broader approach than that of 'psycholinguistics', which is taken to denote the special approach of (Chomskyan) linguistics in co-operation with (neo-behaviouristic) psychology of learning.

3. It should be mentioned that during the period around World War I, many psychologists and educationalists wrote about child development (including child language) on the basis of intensive observation of their own children, or by means of rather 'free' observation of other children, e.g., in nursery schools. One of the most famous contributors not mentioned by Jespersen was Jean Piaget whose first book on child psychology, *Le langage et le pensée chez l'enfant* (1923), will be mentioned in Sections 2 and 3 of this article.
Wilhelm Rasmussen was principal of the Royal Danish School of Educational Studies 1924-39. He was trained as a physicist, but took a special interest in child psychology and education and wrote several books on these topics based upon contemporary psychology as well as upon his observations of his own two daughters.

4. *Nutidssprog*, p. 4.

5. *ibid.*, p. 208.

6. *ibid.*, p. 95ff; *Language*, p. 124ff.

7. The sections on sounds, words, forms and sentences contain 50, 80, 29 and 20 pages, respectively, in *Nutidssprog*,1916.

8. *ibid.*, p. 11; *Language*, p. 103.

9. *ibid.*, p. 18; resp. p. 105.

10. *ibid.*, p. 24.

11. *ibid.*, p. 26.

12. *ibid.*, p. 26.

13. *ibid.*, p. 52; resp. p. 113

14. *ibid.*, p. 56; resp. p. 115.

15. The issues (a)-(i) are dealt with in *Nutidssprog*, pp. 70, 76, 83, 88,

95, 105, 111, 114, 119 and 122. In *Language*, a brief account is presented on pp. 117-26.

16. *Nutidssprog*, pp. 177-92.
17. *Language*, p. 128.
18. *ibid.*, p. 129.
19. *Nutidssprog*, pp. 134-43.
20. *Language*, pp. 131-2.
21. In *Language*, Chapters IX and X are devoted to the theme of 'The Influence of the Child on Linguistic Development'.
22. During the last few decades, psycholinguists as well as sociolinguists have often studied hesitation phenomena.
23. *ibid.*, pp. 132-3.
24. *ibid.*, pp. 3-4.
25. Cf. one of the most famous of the early psycholinguistic studies by Roger Brown and Ursula Bellugi in *Harvard Educational Review*, 1964.
26. *Language*, pp. 137-8.
27. *ibid.*, p. 139.
28. *Linguistics*: M.A.K. Halliday's *Exploration into the Functions of Language* and *Learning How to Mean*, published by E. Arnold in 1973 and 1975, analyze in a very consistent manner the birth of language in children in terms of *functions*: to acquire one's mother tongue implies, above all, the learning of how to *mean*, i.e., how to intend and how to obtain what one intends by means of verbal utterances.

Psychology: Soviet psychologists such as L.S. Vygotsky and A.R. Luria consistently stress the importance of speech for the direction of behaviour and thinking; and Jean Piaget's classical distinction between 'egocentric' and 'socialized' speech is a matter of intention and function.

Philosophy: Most far-reachingly, J.L. Austin's and J.R. Searle's theory of speech acts states that to make an utterance is always to perform an illocutionary act.

29. *ibid.*, p. 134.
30. *ibid.*, pp. 141-4; *Nutidssprog*, pp. 222-32.
31. The explanations criticized are:
    – the child's organs of speech are especially flexible;
    – the child's ears are especially sensitive;
    – the child has no established (bad) habits to contend against;
    – the child has nothing else to do than learning the language.
    ibid., pp. 140-41; *Nutidssprog*, pp. 222-6.
32. *ibid.*, p. 141.
33. Jespersen adds that 'if *men* had to attend to their children they would never use so many words'; *ibid.*, p. 142.
34. In Danish, 'linguistic awareness' is unfortunately often translated in such a way that it may be conceived of as 'linguistic consciousness' or '(reflective) knowledge about language'. In any case, it is often by no means clear whether relatively unreflective *attention* toward linguistic phenomena or reflective *knowledge* about them is the virtual prerequisite of reading and writing. Further, it must be assumed that not only 'linguistic awareness', but also 'communicative awareness' facilitates the acquisition of written language. (Vejleskov: 'Communication vs. Language Disabilities', Paper for the XIXth Congress of The International Ass. of Logopaedics and Phoniatrics, Edinburgh, 1983.)
35. *Nutidssprog*, pp. 21-2, 43-9, 143-7, 193-7; *Language*, pp. 110-11, 130-31, 148-9.
36. *Language*, p. 111.
37. *ibid.*, p. 130.
38. *Nutidssprog*, p. 194.
39. The article (cf. Note 1) is in fact an extract from *Nutidssprog*.
40. This example also appears in *Language*, p. 114.
41. See for instance the chapter by D.E. Rumelhart in *Metaphor and Thought*, ed. by A. Ortony, Cambridge University Press, 1979.
42. See for instance *The Development Psychology of Jean Piaget* by

J.H. Flavell, van Nostrand, 1963.
43. *Language*, p. 127.
44. See for instance D.R. Olson, 'From Utterance to Text', *Harvard Educ. Rev.* 1977.
45. *Nutidssprog*, pp. 265-76.
46. In *How to Teach a Foreign Language* Jespersen clearly advocates a method that at the same time (a) makes the written form correspond as much as possible to the oral form, and (b) to a high degree makes it possible for the pupil to utilize the reading habits acquired in his mother tongue.
47. *Nutidssprog*, pp. 247-50.
48. *Tale, snak og sprog*. Småbøger om småbørn, III. Copenhagen: Pædagogisk-Psykologisk Forlag, 1985.
49. *Nutidssprog*, p. 254.
50. *ibid.*, p. 264.

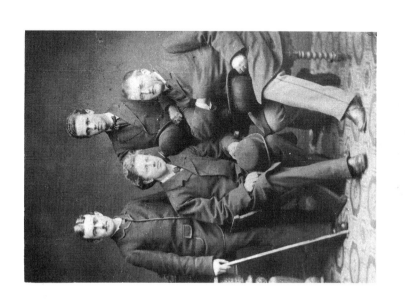

Otto Jespersen (second from left) at Regensen. See pp. 13-14. From a group photograph (Regensen, 1878). By courtesy of Regensen. By courtesy of the Royal Library, Copenhagen.

Otto Jespersen (1887).
By courtesy of the Royal Library, Copenhagen.

Henry Buergel Goodwin. Otto Jespersen (Gentofte 1907).
See pp. xv-xvi.
By courtesy of the Royal Library, Copenhagen.

Otto Jespersen as Rektor (Vice-Chancellor)
of Copenhagen University (1920-21). See p. 21.

Copyright Alfred Müller. Nordisk Pressefoto A/S Copenhagen.

English undergraduate actors visiting Copenhagen University (1923).
Niels Bøgholm (second from left (see p. 19)); Aage Brusendorff (third from left (see p. 19));
Otto Jespersen (centre). By courtesy of the Royal Library, Copenhagen.

Otto Jespersen at Lundehave, Elsinore (1934). See p. 20.
By courtesy of the Royal Library, Copenhagen.

Vagn Guldbrandsen. Otto Jespersen at Lundehave, Elsinore (c. 1939).

By courtesy of Hans P. Guldbrandsen
(Vagn Guldbrandsen Aps.), Copenhagen,
and the Royal Library, Copenhagen.

Royal Photographer Elfelt Royal, Copenhagen. Otto Jespersen (1940).

By courtesy of Royal Photographer Elfelt Royal, Copenhagen, and the Royal Library, Copenhagen.

In the STUDIES IN THE HISTORY OF THE LANGUAGE SCIENCES (SiHoLS) series (Series Editor: E.F. Konrad Koerner) the following volumes have been published thus far, and will be published during 1989:

1. KOERNER, E.F. Konrad: *The Importance of Techmer's "Internationale Zeitschrift für Allgemeine Sprachwissenschaft" in the Development of General Linguistics.* Amsterdam, 1973.

2. TAYLOR, Daniel J.: *Declinatio: A Study of the Linguistic Theory of Marcus Terentius Varro.* Amsterdam, 1974. 2nd pr. 1989.

3. BENWARE, Wilbur A.: *The Study of Indo-European Vocalism; from the beginnings to Whitney and Scherer: A critical-historical account.* Amsterdam, 1974. t.o.p. 2nd pr. 1989.

4. BACHER, Wilhelm: *Die Anfänge der hebräischen Grammatik* (1895), together with *Die hebräische Sprachwissenschaft vom 10. bis zum 16. Jahrhundert* (1892). Amsterdam, 1974.

5. HUNT, R.W. (1908-1979): *The History of Grammar in the Middle Ages. Collected Papers.* Edited with an introduction, a select bibliography, and indices by G.L. Bursill-Hall. Amsterdam, 1980.

6. MILLER, Roy Andrew: *Studies in the Grammatical Tradition in Tibet.* Amsterdam, 1976.

7. PEDERSEN, Holger (1867-1953): *A Glance at the History of Linguistics, with particular regard to the historical study of phonology.* Amsterdam, 1983.

8. STENGEL, Edmund (1845-1935), (ed.): *Chronologisches Verzeichnis französischer Grammatiken vom Ende des 14. bis zum Ausgange des 18. Jahrhunderts, nebst Angabe der bisher ermittelten Fundorte derselben.* Amsterdam, 1976.

9. NIEDEREHE, Hans-Josef & Harald HAARMANN (with the assistance of Liliane Rouday), (eds.): *IN MEMORIAM FRIEDRICH DIEZ: Akten des Kolloquiums zur Wissenschaftsgeschichte der Romanistik/Actes du Colloque sur l'Histoire des Etudes Romanes/Proceedings of the Colloquium for the History of Romance Studies, Trier, 2.-4. Okt. 1975).* Amsterdam, 1976.

10. KILBURY, James: *The Development of Morphophonemic Theory.* Amsterdam, 1976.

11. KOERNER, E.F. Konrad: *Western Histories of Linguistic Thought. An annotated chronological bibliography, 1822-1976.* Amsterdam, 1978.

12. PAULINUS a S. BARTHOLOMAEO (1749-1806): *Dissertation on the Sanskrit Language.* Transl., edited and introduced by Ludo Rocher. Amsterdam, 1977.

13. DRAKE, Glendon F.: *The Role of Prescriptivism in American Linguistics 1820-1970.* Amsterdam, 1977.

14. SIGERUS DE CORTRACO: *Summa modorum significandi; Sophismata.* New edition, on the basis of G. Wallerand's *editio prima,* with additions, critical notes, an index of terms, and an introd. by Jan Pinborg. Amsterdam, 1977.

15. PSEUDO-ALBERTUS MAGNUS: *Quaestiones Alberti de Modis significandi.* A critical edition, translation and commentary of the British Museum Inc. C.21.C.52 and the Cambridge Inc.5.J.3.7, by L.G. Kelly. Amsterdam, 1977.

16. PANCONCELLI-CALZIA, Giulio (1878-1966): *Geschichtszahlen der Phonetik* (1941), together with *Quellenatlas der Phonetik* (1940). New ed., with an introd. article and a bio-bibliographical account of Panconcelli-Calzia by Jens-Peter Köster. Amsterdam, n.y.p.

17. SALMON, Vivian: *The Study of Language in 17th-Century England.* Amsterdam, 1979. Second edition 1988.

18. HAYASHI, Tetsuro: *The Theory of English Lexicography 1530-1791.* Amsterdam, 1978.

19. KOERNER, E.F. Konrad: *Toward a Historiography of Linguistics. Selected Essays.* Foreword by R.H. Robins. Amsterdam, 1978.
20. KOERNER, E.F. Konrad (ed.): *PROGRESS IN LINGUISTIC HISTORIOGRA-PHY: Papers from the International Conference on the History of the Language Sciences, Ottawa, 28-31 August 1978.* Amsterdam, 1980.
21. DAVIS, Boyd H. & Raymond K. O'CAIN (eds.): *FIRST PERSON SINGULAR. Papers from the Conference on an Oral Archive for the History of American Linguistics. (Charlotte, N.C., 9-10 March 1979).* Amsterdam, 1980.
22. McDERMOTT, A. Charlene Senape: *Godfrey of Fontaine's Abridgement of Boethius the Dane's MODI SIGNIFICANDI SIVE QUAESTIONES SUPER PRISCIANUM MAIOREM.* A text edition with English transl. and introd. Amsterdam, 1980.
23. APOLLONIUS DYSCOLUS: *The Syntax of Apollonius Dyscolus.* Translated, and with commentary by Fred W. Householder. Amsterdam, 1981.
24. CARTER, M.. (ed.): *ARAB LINGUISTICS, an introductory classical text with translation and notes.* Amsterdam, 1981.
25. HYMES, Dell H.: *Essays in the History of Linguistic Anthropology.* Amsterdam, 1983.
26. KOERNER, Konrad, Hans-J. NIEDEREHE & R.H. ROBINS (eds.): *STUDIES IN MEDIEVAL LINGUISTIC THOUGHT,* dedicated to Geoffrey L. Bursill-Hall on the occasion of his 60th birthday on 15 May 1980. Amsterdam, 1980.
27. BREVA-CLARAMONTE, Manuel: *Sanctius' Theory of Language: A contribution to the history of Renaissance linguistics.* Amsterdam, 1983.
28. VERSTEEGH, Kees, Konrad KOERNER & Hans-J. NIEDEREHE (eds.): *THE HISTORY OF LINGUISTICS IN THE NEAR EAST.* Amsterdam, 1983.
29. ARENS, Hans: *Aristotle's Theory of Language and its Tradition.* Amsterdam, 1984.
30. GORDON, W. Terrence: *A History of Semantics.* Amsterdam, 1982.
31. CHRISTY, Craig: *Uniformitarianism in Linguistics.* Amsterdam 1983.
32. MANCHESTER, M.L.: *The Philosophical Foundations of Humboldt's Linguistic Doctrines.* Amsterdam 1985.
33. RAMAT, Paolo, Hans-Josef NIEDEREHE & E.F. Konrad KOERNER (eds.): *THE HISTORY OF LINGUISTICS IN ITALY.* Amsterdam, 1986.
34. QUILIS, Antonio & Hans J. NIEDEREHE (eds.): *THE HISTORY OF LINGUISTICS IN SPAIN.* Amsterdam, 1986.
35. SALMON, Vivian & Edwina BURNESS (comps.): *A READER IN THE LANGUAGE OF SHAKESPEAREAN DRAMA.* Amsterdam, 1987.
36. SAPIR, Edward: *Appraisals of his Life and Work.* Edited by Konrad Koerner. Amsterdam, 1984.
37. Ó MATHÚNA, Seán P.: *William Bathe, S.J., 1564-1614: a pioneer in linguistics.* Amsterdam, 1986.
38. AARSLEFF, Hans, Louis G. KELLY & Hans-Josef NIEDEREHE: *PAPERS IN THE HISTORY OF LINGUISTICS. Proceedings of ICHoLS III, Princeton 1984.* Amsterdam, 1987.
39. PETRUS HISPANUS: *Summulae Logicales.* Translated and with an introduction by Francis P. Dinneen, S.J. Amsterdam, 1989. n.y.p.
40. HARTMANN, R.R.K. (ed.): *THE HISTORY OF LEXICOGRAPHY. Papers from the Dictionary Research Centre Seminar at Exeter, March 1986.* Amsterdam, 1986.
41. COWAN, William, Michael K. FOSTER & Konrad KOERNER (eds): *NEW PERSPECTIVES IN LANGUAGE, CULTURE, AND PERSONALITY. Proceedings of the Edward Sapir Centenary Conference (Ottawa, 1-3 October 1984).* Amsterdam, 1986.

42. BUZZETTI, Dino & Maurizio FERRIANI (eds): *SPECULATIVE GRAMMAR, UNIVERSAL GRAMMAR, AND PHILOSOPHICAL ANALYSIS OF LANGUAGE*. Amsterdam, 1987.

43. BURSILL-HALL, G. L., Sten EBBESEN & E.F. Konrad KOERNER (eds): *DE ORTU GRAMMATICAE. Studies in Medieval Grammar and Linguistic Theory in Memory of Jan Pinborg*. Amsterdam/Philadelphia, 1989. n.y.p.

44. AMSLER, Mark: *Etymology and Discourse in Late Antiquity and the Early Middle Ages*. Amsterdam/Philadelphia, 1989.

45. OWENS, Jonathan: *The Foundations of Grammar*. Amsterdam, 1987.

46. TAYLOR, Daniel (ed.): *THE HISTORY OF LINGUISTICS IN THE CLASSICAL PERIOD*. Amsterdam, 1987.

47. HALL, Robert A. jr. (ed.): *LEONARD BLOOMFIELD, ESSAYS ON HIS LIFE AND WORK*. Amsterdam, 1987.

48. FORMIGARI, Lia: *Language and Experience in 17th-century British Philosophy*. Amsterdam/Philadelphia, 1989.

49. DE MAURO, Tullio & Lia FORMIGARI: *Leibniz, Humboldt, and the Origins of Comparativism. Proceedings of the international conference, Rome, 25-28 September 1986*. Amsterdam/Philadelphia, 1989. n.y.p.

50. KOERNER, Konrad: *Practicing Linguistic Historiography. Selected Essays*. Amsterdam/Philadelphia, 1989.

51. KOERNER, Konrad & Hans-Josef NIEDEREHE (eds): *History and Historiography of Linguistics*. Amsterdam/Philadelphia, 1989. n.y.p.

52. JUUL, Arne & Hans F. NIELSEN (eds): *Otto Jespersen: Facets of his Life and Work*. Amsterdam/Philadelphia, 1989.